C-2906 CAREER EXAMINATION SERIES

This is your
PASSBOOK for...

Youth Counselor

**Test Preparation Study Guide
Questions & Answers**

COPYRIGHT NOTICE

This book is SOLELY intended for, is sold ONLY to, and its use is RESTRICTED to individual, bona fide applicants or candidates who qualify by virtue of having seriously filed applications for appropriate license, certificate, professional and/or promotional advancement, higher school matriculation, scholarship, or other legitimate requirements of education and/or governmental authorities.

This book is NOT intended for use, class instruction, tutoring, training, duplication, copying, reprinting, excerption, or adaptation, etc., by:

1) Other publishers
2) Proprietors and/or Instructors of "Coaching" and/or Preparatory Courses
3) Personnel and/or Training Divisions of commercial, industrial, and governmental organizations
4) Schools, colleges, or universities and/or their departments and staffs, including teachers and other personnel
5) Testing Agencies or Bureaus
6) Study groups which seek by the purchase of a single volume to copy and/or duplicate and/or adapt this material for use by the group as a whole without having purchased individual volumes for each of the members of the group
7) Et al.

Such persons would be in violation of appropriate Federal and State statutes.

PROVISION OF LICENSING AGREEMENTS – Recognized educational, commercial, industrial, and governmental institutions and organizations, and others legitimately engaged in educational pursuits, including training, testing, and measurement activities, may address request for a licensing agreement to the copyright owners, who will determine whether, and under what conditions, including fees and charges, the materials in this book may be used them. In other words, a licensing facility exists for the legitimate use of the material in this book on other than an individual basis. However, it is asseverated and affirmed here that the material in this book CANNOT be used without the receipt of the express permission of such a licensing agreement from the Publishers. Inquiries re licensing should be addressed to the company, attention rights and permissions department.

All rights reserved, including the right of reproduction in whole or in part, in any form or by any means, electronic or mechanical, including photocopying, recording, or by any information storage and retrieval system, without permission in writing from the Publisher.

Copyright © 2024 by
National Learning Corporation

212 Michael Drive, Syosset, NY 11791
(516) 921-8888 • www.passbooks.com
E-mail: info@passbooks.com

PUBLISHED IN THE UNITED STATES OF AMERICA

PASSBOOK® SERIES

THE *PASSBOOK® SERIES* has been created to prepare applicants and candidates for the ultimate academic battlefield – the examination room.

At some time in our lives, each and every one of us may be required to take an examination – for validation, matriculation, admission, qualification, registration, certification, or licensure.

Based on the assumption that every applicant or candidate has met the basic formal educational standards, has taken the required number of courses, and read the necessary texts, the *PASSBOOK® SERIES* furnishes the one special preparation which may assure passing with confidence, instead of failing with insecurity. Examination questions – together with answers – are furnished as the basic vehicle for study so that the mysteries of the examination and its compounding difficulties may be eliminated or diminished by a sure method.

This book is meant to help you pass your examination provided that you qualify and are serious in your objective.

The entire field is reviewed through the huge store of content information which is succinctly presented through a provocative and challenging approach – the question-and-answer method.

A climate of success is established by furnishing the correct answers at the end of each test.

You soon learn to recognize types of questions, forms of questions, and patterns of questioning. You may even begin to anticipate expected outcomes.

You perceive that many questions are repeated or adapted so that you can gain acute insights, which may enable you to score many sure points.

You learn how to confront new questions, or types of questions, and to attack them confidently and work out the correct answers.

You note objectives and emphases, and recognize pitfalls and dangers, so that you may make positive educational adjustments.

Moreover, you are kept fully informed in relation to new concepts, methods, practices, and directions in the field.

You discover that you are actually taking the examination all the time: you are preparing for the examination by "taking" an examination, not by reading extraneous and/or supererogatory textbooks.

In short, this PASSBOOK®, used directedly, should be an important factor in helping you to pass your test.

YOUTH COUNSELOR

DUTIES:

As a **Youth Counselor,** you would be responsible for supervising, evaluating, guiding, and the case management of juvenile and youthful offenders, juvenile delinquents, or other trouble prone youth placed with the Office of Children and Family Services. Your actual duties may vary depending on the setting to which you are assigned, including secure, limited secure, or non-secure residential centers, community foster care, intake services units, evening reporting centers and aftercare teams in the community. You would be expected to promote and maintain a structured environment and be able to physically restrain youth, if required. Training on restraints will be required, and will be provided by the agency as part of the probationary period. Refresher training will also be provided by the agency every year. Duties might also include maintaining facility security and personal safety; interaction with other agencies, families, and schools; and placement of youth in appropriate treatment programs in the community; and supervision of Youth Division Aides.

SUBJECT OF EXAMINATION:

The written test is designed to test for knowledge, skills, and/or abilities in such areas as:

1. **Adolescent development** - These questions test for knowledge of the principles, practices, and problems of adolescent growth and development. Questions may cover such topics as recognizing behavioral patterns of normal adolescent development; understanding the causes of problem behavior in adolescents; identifying the effects of family, school, peers, and other influences on adolescent behavior; and understanding the culture, values, and lifestyles of educationally, socially, and economically disadvantaged youth.
2. **Preparing written material** - These questions test for the ability to present information clearly and accurately, and to organize paragraphs logically and comprehensibly. For some questions, you will be given information in two or three sentences followed by four restatements of the information. You must then choose the best version. For other questions, you will be given paragraphs with their sentences out of order. You must then choose, from four suggestions, the best order for the sentences.
3. **Principles and practices of therapeutic counseling of court-placed offending youth** - These questions will be designed to test your knowledge, skills and abilities related to guiding and supervising court-placed delinquent youth in a variety of settings and programs, both in the community and in residential rehabilitation facilities. Questions may cover treatment plans, guiding youths and their families, and community and professional relations.
4. **Understanding and interpreting written material** - These questions test how well you comprehend written material. You will be provided with brief reading selections and will be asked questions about the selections. All the information required to answer the questions will be presented in the selections; you will not be required to have any special knowledge relating to the subject areas of the selections.

HOW TO TAKE A TEST

I. YOU MUST PASS AN EXAMINATION

A. *WHAT EVERY CANDIDATE SHOULD KNOW*

Examination applicants often ask us for help in preparing for the written test. What can I study in advance? What kinds of questions will be asked? How will the test be given? How will the papers be graded?

As an applicant for a civil service examination, you may be wondering about some of these things. Our purpose here is to suggest effective methods of advance study and to describe civil service examinations.

Your chances for success on this examination can be increased if you know how to prepare. Those "pre-examination jitters" can be reduced if you know what to expect. You can even experience an adventure in good citizenship if you know why civil service exams are given.

B. *WHY ARE CIVIL SERVICE EXAMINATIONS GIVEN?*

Civil service examinations are important to you in two ways. As a citizen, you want public jobs filled by employees who know how to do their work. As a job seeker, you want a fair chance to compete for that job on an equal footing with other candidates. The best-known means of accomplishing this two-fold goal is the competitive examination.

Exams are widely publicized throughout the nation. They may be administered for jobs in federal, state, city, municipal, town or village governments or agencies.

Any citizen may apply, with some limitations, such as the age or residence of applicants. Your experience and education may be reviewed to see whether you meet the requirements for the particular examination. When these requirements exist, they are reasonable and applied consistently to all applicants. Thus, a competitive examination may cause you some uneasiness now, but it is your privilege and safeguard.

C. *HOW ARE CIVIL SERVICE EXAMS DEVELOPED?*

Examinations are carefully written by trained technicians who are specialists in the field known as "psychological measurement," in consultation with recognized authorities in the field of work that the test will cover. These experts recommend the subject matter areas or skills to be tested; only those knowledges or skills important to your success on the job are included. The most reliable books and source materials available are used as references. Together, the experts and technicians judge the difficulty level of the questions.

Test technicians know how to phrase questions so that the problem is clearly stated. Their ethics do not permit "trick" or "catch" questions. Questions may have been tried out on sample groups, or subjected to statistical analysis, to determine their usefulness.

Written tests are often used in combination with performance tests, ratings of training and experience, and oral interviews. All of these measures combine to form the best-known means of finding the right person for the right job.

II. HOW TO PASS THE WRITTEN TEST

A. NATURE OF THE EXAMINATION

To prepare intelligently for civil service examinations, you should know how they differ from school examinations you have taken. In school you were assigned certain definite pages to read or subjects to cover. The examination questions were quite detailed and usually emphasized memory. Civil service exams, on the other hand, try to discover your present ability to perform the duties of a position, plus your potentiality to learn these duties. In other words, a civil service exam attempts to predict how successful you will be. Questions cover such a broad area that they cannot be as minute and detailed as school exam questions.

In the public service similar kinds of work, or positions, are grouped together in one "class." This process is known as *position-classification*. All the positions in a class are paid according to the salary range for that class. One class title covers all of these positions, and they are all tested by the same examination.

B. FOUR BASIC STEPS

1) Study the announcement

How, then, can you know what subjects to study? Our best answer is: "Learn as much as possible about the class of positions for which you've applied." The exam will test the knowledge, skills and abilities needed to do the work.

Your most valuable source of information about the position you want is the official exam announcement. This announcement lists the training and experience qualifications. Check these standards and apply only if you come reasonably close to meeting them.

The brief description of the position in the examination announcement offers some clues to the subjects which will be tested. Think about the job itself. Review the duties in your mind. Can you perform them, or are there some in which you are rusty? Fill in the blank spots in your preparation.

Many jurisdictions preview the written test in the exam announcement by including a section called "Knowledge and Abilities Required," "Scope of the Examination," or some similar heading. Here you will find out specifically what fields will be tested.

2) Review your own background

Once you learn in general what the position is all about, and what you need to know to do the work, ask yourself which subjects you already know fairly well and which need improvement. You may wonder whether to concentrate on improving your strong areas or on building some background in your fields of weakness. When the announcement has specified "some knowledge" or "considerable knowledge," or has used adjectives like "beginning principles of..." or "advanced ... methods," you can get a clue as to the number and difficulty of questions to be asked in any given field. More questions, and hence broader coverage, would be included for those subjects which are more important in the work. Now weigh your strengths and weaknesses against the job requirements and prepare accordingly.

3) Determine the level of the position

Another way to tell how intensively you should prepare is to understand the level of the job for which you are applying. Is it the entering level? In other words, is this the position in which beginners in a field of work are hired? Or is it an intermediate or advanced level? Sometimes this is indicated by such words as "Junior" or "Senior" in the class title. Other jurisdictions use Roman numerals to designate the level – Clerk I, Clerk II, for example. The word "Supervisor" sometimes appears in the title. If the level is not indicated by the title, check the description of duties. Will you be working under very close supervision, or will you have responsibility for independent decisions in this work?

4) Choose appropriate study materials

Now that you know the subjects to be examined and the relative amount of each subject to be covered, you can choose suitable study materials. For beginning level jobs, or even advanced ones, if you have a pronounced weakness in some aspect of your training, read a modern, standard textbook in that field. Be sure it is up to date and has general coverage. Such books are normally available at your library, and the librarian will be glad to help you locate one. For entry-level positions, questions of appropriate difficulty are chosen – neither highly advanced questions, nor those too simple. Such questions require careful thought but not advanced training.

If the position for which you are applying is technical or advanced, you will read more advanced, specialized material. If you are already familiar with the basic principles of your field, elementary textbooks would waste your time. Concentrate on advanced textbooks and technical periodicals. Think through the concepts and review difficult problems in your field.

These are all general sources. You can get more ideas on your own initiative, following these leads. For example, training manuals and publications of the government agency which employs workers in your field can be useful, particularly for technical and professional positions. A letter or visit to the government department involved may result in more specific study suggestions, and certainly will provide you with a more definite idea of the exact nature of the position you are seeking.

III. KINDS OF TESTS

Tests are used for purposes other than measuring knowledge and ability to perform specified duties. For some positions, it is equally important to test ability to make adjustments to new situations or to profit from training. In others, basic mental abilities not dependent on information are essential. Questions which test these things may not appear as pertinent to the duties of the position as those which test for knowledge and information. Yet they are often highly important parts of a fair examination. For very general questions, it is almost impossible to help you direct your study efforts. What we can do is to point out some of the more common of these general abilities needed in public service positions and describe some typical questions.

1) General information

Broad, general information has been found useful for predicting job success in some kinds of work. This is tested in a variety of ways, from vocabulary lists to questions about current events. Basic background in some field of work, such as sociology or economics, may be sampled in a group of questions. Often these are principles which have become familiar to most persons through exposure rather than through formal training. It is difficult to advise you how to study for these questions; being alert to the world around you is our best suggestion.

2) Verbal ability

An example of an ability needed in many positions is verbal or language ability. Verbal ability is, in brief, the ability to use and understand words. Vocabulary and grammar tests are typical measures of this ability. Reading comprehension or paragraph interpretation questions are common in many kinds of civil service tests. You are given a paragraph of written material and asked to find its central meaning.

3) Numerical ability

Number skills can be tested by the familiar arithmetic problem, by checking paired lists of numbers to see which are alike and which are different, or by interpreting charts and graphs. In the latter test, a graph may be printed in the test booklet which you are asked to use as the basis for answering questions.

4) Observation

A popular test for law-enforcement positions is the observation test. A picture is shown to you for several minutes, then taken away. Questions about the picture test your ability to observe both details and larger elements.

5) Following directions

In many positions in the public service, the employee must be able to carry out written instructions dependably and accurately. You may be given a chart with several columns, each column listing a variety of information. The questions require you to carry out directions involving the information given in the chart.

6) Skills and aptitudes

Performance tests effectively measure some manual skills and aptitudes. When the skill is one in which you are trained, such as typing or shorthand, you can practice. These tests are often very much like those given in business school or high school courses. For many of the other skills and aptitudes, however, no short-time preparation can be made. Skills and abilities natural to you or that you have developed throughout your lifetime are being tested.

Many of the general questions just described provide all the data needed to answer the questions and ask you to use your reasoning ability to find the answers. Your best preparation for these tests, as well as for tests of facts and ideas, is to be at your physical and mental best. You, no doubt, have your own methods of getting into an exam-taking mood and keeping "in shape." The next section lists some ideas on this subject.

IV. KINDS OF QUESTIONS

Only rarely is the "essay" question, which you answer in narrative form, used in civil service tests. Civil service tests are usually of the short-answer type. Full instructions for answering these questions will be given to you at the examination. But in case this is your first experience with short-answer questions and separate answer sheets, here is what you need to know:

1) Multiple-choice Questions

Most popular of the short-answer questions is the "multiple choice" or "best answer" question. It can be used, for example, to test for factual knowledge, ability to solve problems or judgment in meeting situations found at work.

A multiple-choice question is normally one of three types—
- It can begin with an incomplete statement followed by several possible endings. You are to find the one ending which *best* completes the statement, although some of the others may not be entirely wrong.
- It can also be a complete statement in the form of a question which is answered by choosing one of the statements listed.

- It can be in the form of a problem – again you select the best answer.

Here is an example of a multiple-choice question with a discussion which should give you some clues as to the method for choosing the right answer:

When an employee has a complaint about his assignment, the action which will *best* help him overcome his difficulty is to
- A. discuss his difficulty with his coworkers
- B. take the problem to the head of the organization
- C. take the problem to the person who gave him the assignment
- D. say nothing to anyone about his complaint

In answering this question, you should study each of the choices to find which is best. Consider choice "A" – Certainly an employee may discuss his complaint with fellow employees, but no change or improvement can result, and the complaint remains unresolved. Choice "B" is a poor choice since the head of the organization probably does not know what assignment you have been given, and taking your problem to him is known as "going over the head" of the supervisor. The supervisor, or person who made the assignment, is the person who can clarify it or correct any injustice. Choice "C" is, therefore, correct. To say nothing, as in choice "D," is unwise. Supervisors have and interest in knowing the problems employees are facing, and the employee is seeking a solution to his problem.

2) True/False Questions

The "true/false" or "right/wrong" form of question is sometimes used. Here a complete statement is given. Your job is to decide whether the statement is right or wrong.

SAMPLE: A roaming cell-phone call to a nearby city costs less than a non-roaming call to a distant city.

This statement is wrong, or false, since roaming calls are more expensive.

This is not a complete list of all possible question forms, although most of the others are variations of these common types. You will always get complete directions for answering questions. Be sure you understand *how* to mark your answers – ask questions until you do.

V. RECORDING YOUR ANSWERS

Computer terminals are used more and more today for many different kinds of exams.

For an examination with very few applicants, you may be told to record your answers in the test booklet itself. Separate answer sheets are much more common. If this separate answer sheet is to be scored by machine – and this is often the case – it is highly important that you mark your answers correctly in order to get credit.

An electronic scoring machine is often used in civil service offices because of the speed with which papers can be scored. Machine-scored answer sheets must be marked with a pencil, which will be given to you. This pencil has a high graphite content which responds to the electronic scoring machine. As a matter of fact, stray dots may register as answers, so do not let your pencil rest on the answer sheet while you are pondering the correct answer. Also, if your pencil lead breaks or is otherwise defective, ask for another.

Since the answer sheet will be dropped in a slot in the scoring machine, be careful not to bend the corners or get the paper crumpled.

The answer sheet normally has five vertical columns of numbers, with 30 numbers to a column. These numbers correspond to the question numbers in your test booklet. After each number, going across the page are four or five pairs of dotted lines. These short dotted lines have small letters or numbers above them. The first two pairs may also have a "T" or "F" above the letters. This indicates that the first two pairs only are to be used if the questions are of the true-false type. If the questions are multiple choice, disregard the "T" and "F" and pay attention only to the small letters or numbers.

Answer your questions in the manner of the sample that follows:

32. The largest city in the United States is
    A. Washington, D.C.
    B. New York City
    C. Chicago
    D. Detroit
    E. San Francisco

1) Choose the answer you think is best. (New York City is the largest, so "B" is correct.)
2) Find the row of dotted lines numbered the same as the question you are answering. (Find row number 32)
3) Find the pair of dotted lines corresponding to the answer. (Find the pair of lines under the mark "B.")
4) Make a solid black mark between the dotted lines.

VI. BEFORE THE TEST

Common sense will help you find procedures to follow to get ready for an examination. Too many of us, however, overlook these sensible measures. Indeed, nervousness and fatigue have been found to be the most serious reasons why applicants fail to do their best on civil service tests. Here is a list of reminders:

- Begin your preparation early – Don't wait until the last minute to go scurrying around for books and materials or to find out what the position is all about.
- Prepare continuously – An hour a night for a week is better than an all-night cram session. This has been definitely established. What is more, a night a week for a month will return better dividends than crowding your study into a shorter period of time.
- Locate the place of the exam – You have been sent a notice telling you when and where to report for the examination. If the location is in a different town or otherwise unfamiliar to you, it would be well to inquire the best route and learn something about the building.
- Relax the night before the test – Allow your mind to rest. Do not study at all that night. Plan some mild recreation or diversion; then go to bed early and get a good night's sleep.
- Get up early enough to make a leisurely trip to the place for the test – This way unforeseen events, traffic snarls, unfamiliar buildings, etc. will not upset you.
- Dress comfortably – A written test is not a fashion show. You will be known by number and not by name, so wear something comfortable.

- Leave excess paraphernalia at home – Shopping bags and odd bundles will get in your way. You need bring only the items mentioned in the official notice you received; usually everything you need is provided. Do not bring reference books to the exam. They will only confuse those last minutes and be taken away from you when in the test room.
- Arrive somewhat ahead of time – If because of transportation schedules you must get there very early, bring a newspaper or magazine to take your mind off yourself while waiting.
- Locate the examination room – When you have found the proper room, you will be directed to the seat or part of the room where you will sit. Sometimes you are given a sheet of instructions to read while you are waiting. Do not fill out any forms until you are told to do so; just read them and be prepared.
- Relax and prepare to listen to the instructions
- If you have any physical problem that may keep you from doing your best, be sure to tell the test administrator. If you are sick or in poor health, you really cannot do your best on the exam. You can come back and take the test some other time.

VII. AT THE TEST

The day of the test is here and you have the test booklet in your hand. The temptation to get going is very strong. Caution! There is more to success than knowing the right answers. You must know how to identify your papers and understand variations in the type of short-answer question used in this particular examination. Follow these suggestions for maximum results from your efforts:

1) Cooperate with the monitor

The test administrator has a duty to create a situation in which you can be as much at ease as possible. He will give instructions, tell you when to begin, check to see that you are marking your answer sheet correctly, and so on. He is not there to guard you, although he will see that your competitors do not take unfair advantage. He wants to help you do your best.

2) Listen to all instructions

Don't jump the gun! Wait until you understand all directions. In most civil service tests you get more time than you need to answer the questions. So don't be in a hurry. Read each word of instructions until you clearly understand the meaning. Study the examples, listen to all announcements and follow directions. Ask questions if you do not understand what to do.

3) Identify your papers

Civil service exams are usually identified by number only. You will be assigned a number; you must not put your name on your test papers. Be sure to copy your number correctly. Since more than one exam may be given, copy your exact examination title.

4) Plan your time

Unless you are told that a test is a "speed" or "rate of work" test, speed itself is usually not important. Time enough to answer all the questions will be provided, but this does not mean that you have all day. An overall time limit has been set. Divide the total time (in minutes) by the number of questions to determine the approximate time you have for each question.

5) Do not linger over difficult questions

If you come across a difficult question, mark it with a paper clip (useful to have along) and come back to it when you have been through the booklet. One caution if you do this – be sure to skip a number on your answer sheet as well. Check often to be sure that you have not lost your place and that you are marking in the row numbered the same as the question you are answering.

6) Read the questions

Be sure you know what the question asks! Many capable people are unsuccessful because they failed to *read* the questions correctly.

7) Answer all questions

Unless you have been instructed that a penalty will be deducted for incorrect answers, it is better to guess than to omit a question.

8) Speed tests

It is often better NOT to guess on speed tests. It has been found that on timed tests people are tempted to spend the last few seconds before time is called in marking answers at random – without even reading them – in the hope of picking up a few extra points. To discourage this practice, the instructions may warn you that your score will be "corrected" for guessing. That is, a penalty will be applied. The incorrect answers will be deducted from the correct ones, or some other penalty formula will be used.

9) Review your answers

If you finish before time is called, go back to the questions you guessed or omitted to give them further thought. Review other answers if you have time.

10) Return your test materials

If you are ready to leave before others have finished or time is called, take ALL your materials to the monitor and leave quietly. Never take any test material with you. The monitor can discover whose papers are not complete, and taking a test booklet may be grounds for disqualification.

VIII. EXAMINATION TECHNIQUES

1) Read the general instructions carefully. These are usually printed on the first page of the exam booklet. As a rule, these instructions refer to the timing of the examination; the fact that you should not start work until the signal and must stop work at a signal, etc. If there are any *special* instructions, such as a choice of questions to be answered, make sure that you note this instruction carefully.

2) When you are ready to start work on the examination, that is as soon as the signal has been given, read the instructions to each question booklet, underline any key words or phrases, such as *least, best, outline, describe* and the like. In this way you will tend to answer as requested rather than discover on reviewing your paper that you *listed without describing*, that you selected the *worst* choice rather than the *best* choice, etc.

3) If the examination is of the objective or multiple-choice type – that is, each question will also give a series of possible answers: A, B, C or D, and you are called upon to select the best answer and write the letter next to that answer on your answer paper – it is advisable to start answering each question in turn. There may be anywhere from 50 to 100 such questions in the three or four hours allotted and you can see how much time would be taken if you read through all the questions before beginning to answer any. Furthermore, if you come across a question or group of questions which you know would be difficult to answer, it would undoubtedly affect your handling of all the other questions.

4) If the examination is of the essay type and contains but a few questions, it is a moot point as to whether you should read all the questions before starting to answer any one. Of course, if you are given a choice – say five out of seven and the like – then it is essential to read all the questions so you can eliminate the two that are most difficult. If, however, you are asked to answer all the questions, there may be danger in trying to answer the easiest one first because you may find that you will spend too much time on it. The best technique is to answer the first question, then proceed to the second, etc.

5) Time your answers. Before the exam begins, write down the time it started, then add the time allowed for the examination and write down the time it must be completed, then divide the time available somewhat as follows:
    - If 3-1/2 hours are allowed, that would be 210 minutes. If you have 80 objective-type questions, that would be an average of 2-1/2 minutes per question. Allow yourself no more than 2 minutes per question, or a total of 160 minutes, which will permit about 50 minutes to review.
    - If for the time allotment of 210 minutes there are 7 essay questions to answer, that would average about 30 minutes a question. Give yourself only 25 minutes per question so that you have about 35 minutes to review.

6) The most important instruction is to *read each question* and make sure you know what is wanted. The second most important instruction is to *time yourself properly* so that you answer every question. The third most important instruction is to *answer every question*. Guess if you have to but include something for each question. Remember that you will receive no credit for a blank and will probably receive some credit if you write something in answer to an essay question. If you guess a letter – say "B" for a multiple-choice question – you may have guessed right. If you leave a blank as an answer to a multiple-choice question, the examiners may respect your feelings but it will not add a point to your score. Some exams may penalize you for wrong answers, so in such cases *only*, you may not want to guess unless you have some basis for your answer.

7) Suggestions
    a. Objective-type questions
        1. Examine the question booklet for proper sequence of pages and questions
        2. Read all instructions carefully
        3. Skip any question which seems too difficult; return to it after all other questions have been answered
        4. Apportion your time properly; do not spend too much time on any single question or group of questions

5. Note and underline key words – *all, most, fewest, least, best, worst, same, opposite*, etc.
6. Pay particular attention to negatives
7. Note unusual option, e.g., unduly long, short, complex, different or similar in content to the body of the question
8. Observe the use of "hedging" words – *probably, may, most likely*, etc.
9. Make sure that your answer is put next to the same number as the question
10. Do not second-guess unless you have good reason to believe the second answer is definitely more correct
11. Cross out original answer if you decide another answer is more accurate; do not erase until you are ready to hand your paper in
12. Answer all questions; guess unless instructed otherwise
13. Leave time for review

  b. Essay questions
1. Read each question carefully
2. Determine exactly what is wanted. Underline key words or phrases.
3. Decide on outline or paragraph answer
4. Include many different points and elements unless asked to develop any one or two points or elements
5. Show impartiality by giving pros and cons unless directed to select one side only
6. Make and write down any assumptions you find necessary to answer the questions
7. Watch your English, grammar, punctuation and choice of words
8. Time your answers; don't crowd material

8) Answering the essay question

Most essay questions can be answered by framing the specific response around several key words or ideas. Here are a few such key words or ideas:

M's: manpower, materials, methods, money, management
P's: purpose, program, policy, plan, procedure, practice, problems, pitfalls, personnel, public relations

  a. Six basic steps in handling problems:
1. Preliminary plan and background development
2. Collect information, data and facts
3. Analyze and interpret information, data and facts
4. Analyze and develop solutions as well as make recommendations
5. Prepare report and sell recommendations
6. Install recommendations and follow up effectiveness

  b. Pitfalls to avoid
1. *Taking things for granted* – A statement of the situation does not necessarily imply that each of the elements is necessarily true; for example, a complaint may be invalid and biased so that all that can be taken for granted is that a complaint has been registered

2. *Considering only one side of a situation* – Wherever possible, indicate several alternatives and then point out the reasons you selected the best one
3. *Failing to indicate follow up* – Whenever your answer indicates action on your part, make certain that you will take proper follow-up action to see how successful your recommendations, procedures or actions turn out to be
4. *Taking too long in answering any single question* – Remember to time your answers properly

IX. AFTER THE TEST

Scoring procedures differ in detail among civil service jurisdictions although the general principles are the same. Whether the papers are hand-scored or graded by machine we have described, they are nearly always graded by number. That is, the person who marks the paper knows only the number – never the name – of the applicant. Not until all the papers have been graded will they be matched with names. If other tests, such as training and experience or oral interview ratings have been given, scores will be combined. Different parts of the examination usually have different weights. For example, the written test might count 60 percent of the final grade, and a rating of training and experience 40 percent. In many jurisdictions, veterans will have a certain number of points added to their grades.

After the final grade has been determined, the names are placed in grade order and an eligible list is established. There are various methods for resolving ties between those who get the same final grade – probably the most common is to place first the name of the person whose application was received first. Job offers are made from the eligible list in the order the names appear on it. You will be notified of your grade and your rank as soon as all these computations have been made. This will be done as rapidly as possible.

People who are found to meet the requirements in the announcement are called "eligibles." Their names are put on a list of eligible candidates. An eligible's chances of getting a job depend on how high he stands on this list and how fast agencies are filling jobs from the list.

When a job is to be filled from a list of eligibles, the agency asks for the names of people on the list of eligibles for that job. When the civil service commission receives this request, it sends to the agency the names of the three people highest on this list. Or, if the job to be filled has specialized requirements, the office sends the agency the names of the top three persons who meet these requirements from the general list.

The appointing officer makes a choice from among the three people whose names were sent to him. If the selected person accepts the appointment, the names of the others are put back on the list to be considered for future openings.

That is the rule in hiring from all kinds of eligible lists, whether they are for typist, carpenter, chemist, or something else. For every vacancy, the appointing officer has his choice of any one of the top three eligibles on the list. This explains why the person whose name is on top of the list sometimes does not get an appointment when some of the persons lower on the list do. If the appointing officer chooses the second or third eligible, the No. 1 eligible does not get a job at once, but stays on the list until he is appointed or the list is terminated.

X. HOW TO PASS THE INTERVIEW TEST

The examination for which you applied requires an oral interview test. You have already taken the written test and you are now being called for the interview test – the final part of the formal examination.

You may think that it is not possible to prepare for an interview test and that there are no procedures to follow during an interview. Our purpose is to point out some things you can do in advance that will help you and some good rules to follow and pitfalls to avoid while you are being interviewed.

What is an interview supposed to test?

The written examination is designed to test the technical knowledge and competence of the candidate; the oral is designed to evaluate intangible qualities, not readily measured otherwise, and to establish a list showing the relative fitness of each candidate – as measured against his competitors – for the position sought. Scoring is not on the basis of "right" and "wrong," but on a sliding scale of values ranging from "not passable" to "outstanding." As a matter of fact, it is possible to achieve a relatively low score without a single "incorrect" answer because of evident weakness in the qualities being measured.

Occasionally, an examination may consist entirely of an oral test – either an individual or a group oral. In such cases, information is sought concerning the technical knowledges and abilities of the candidate, since there has been no written examination for this purpose. More commonly, however, an oral test is used to supplement a written examination.

Who conducts interviews?

The composition of oral boards varies among different jurisdictions. In nearly all, a representative of the personnel department serves as chairman. One of the members of the board may be a representative of the department in which the candidate would work. In some cases, "outside experts" are used, and, frequently, a businessman or some other representative of the general public is asked to serve. Labor and management or other special groups may be represented. The aim is to secure the services of experts in the appropriate field.

However the board is composed, it is a good idea (and not at all improper or unethical) to ascertain in advance of the interview who the members are and what groups they represent. When you are introduced to them, you will have some idea of their backgrounds and interests, and at least you will not stutter and stammer over their names.

What should be done before the interview?

While knowledge about the board members is useful and takes some of the surprise element out of the interview, there is other preparation which is more substantive. It *is* possible to prepare for an oral interview – in several ways:

1) Keep a copy of your application and review it carefully before the interview

This may be the only document before the oral board, and the starting point of the interview. Know what education and experience you have listed there, and the sequence and dates of all of it. Sometimes the board will ask you to review the highlights of your experience for them; you should not have to hem and haw doing it.

2) Study the class specification and the examination announcement

Usually, the oral board has one or both of these to guide them. The qualities, characteristics or knowledges required by the position sought are stated in these documents. They offer valuable clues as to the nature of the oral interview. For example, if the job involves supervisory responsibilities, the announcement will usually indicate that knowledge of modern supervisory methods and the qualifications of the candidate as a supervisor will be tested. If so, you can expect such questions, frequently in the form of a hypothetical situation which you are expected to solve. NEVER go into an oral without knowledge of the duties and responsibilities of the job you seek.

3) Think through each qualification required

Try to visualize the kind of questions you would ask if you were a board member. How well could you answer them? Try especially to appraise your own knowledge and background in each area, *measured against the job sought*, and identify any areas in which you are weak. Be critical and realistic – do not flatter yourself.

4) Do some general reading in areas in which you feel you may be weak

For example, if the job involves supervision and your past experience has NOT, some general reading in supervisory methods and practices, particularly in the field of human relations, might be useful. Do NOT study agency procedures or detailed manuals. The oral board will be testing your understanding and capacity, not your memory.

5) Get a good night's sleep and watch your general health and mental attitude

You will want a clear head at the interview. Take care of a cold or any other minor ailment, and of course, no hangovers.

What should be done on the day of the interview?

Now comes the day of the interview itself. Give yourself plenty of time to get there. Plan to arrive somewhat ahead of the scheduled time, particularly if your appointment is in the fore part of the day. If a previous candidate fails to appear, the board might be ready for you a bit early. By early afternoon an oral board is almost invariably behind schedule if there are many candidates, and you may have to wait. Take along a book or magazine to read, or your application to review, but leave any extraneous material in the waiting room when you go in for your interview. In any event, relax and compose yourself.

The matter of dress is important. The board is forming impressions about you – from your experience, your manners, your attitude, and your appearance. Give your personal appearance careful attention. Dress your best, but not your flashiest. Choose conservative, appropriate clothing, and be sure it is immaculate. This is a business interview, and your appearance should indicate that you regard it as such. Besides, being well groomed and properly dressed will help boost your confidence.

Sooner or later, someone will call your name and escort you into the interview room. *This is it.* From here on you are on your own. It is too late for any more preparation. But remember, you asked for this opportunity to prove your fitness, and you are here because your request was granted.

What happens when you go in?

The usual sequence of events will be as follows: The clerk (who is often the board stenographer) will introduce you to the chairman of the oral board, who will introduce you to the other members of the board. Acknowledge the introductions before you sit down. Do not be surprised if you find a microphone facing you or a stenotypist sitting by. Oral interviews are usually recorded in the event of an appeal or other review.

Usually the chairman of the board will open the interview by reviewing the highlights of your education and work experience from your application – primarily for the benefit of the other members of the board, as well as to get the material into the record. Do not interrupt or comment unless there is an error or significant misinterpretation; if that is the case, do not hesitate. But do not quibble about insignificant matters. Also, he will usually ask you some question about your education, experience or your present job – partly to get you to start talking and to establish the interviewing "rapport." He may start the actual questioning, or turn it over to one of the other members. Frequently, each member undertakes the questioning on a particular area, one in which he is perhaps most competent, so you can expect each member to participate in the examination. Because time is limited, you may also expect some rather abrupt switches in the direction the questioning takes, so do not be upset by it. Normally, a board member will not pursue a single line of questioning unless he discovers a particular strength or weakness.

After each member has participated, the chairman will usually ask whether any member has any further questions, then will ask you if you have anything you wish to add. Unless you are expecting this question, it may floor you. Worse, it may start you off on an extended, extemporaneous speech. The board is not usually seeking more information. The question is principally to offer you a last opportunity to present further qualifications or to indicate that you have nothing to add. So, if you feel that a significant qualification or characteristic has been overlooked, it is proper to point it out in a sentence or so. Do not compliment the board on the thoroughness of their examination – they have been sketchy, and you know it. If you wish, merely say, "No thank you, I have nothing further to add." This is a point where you can "talk yourself out" of a good impression or fail to present an important bit of information. Remember, *you close the interview yourself*.

The chairman will then say, "That is all, Mr. _____, thank you." Do not be startled; the interview is over, and quicker than you think. Thank him, gather your belongings and take your leave. Save your sigh of relief for the other side of the door.

How to put your best foot forward

Throughout this entire process, you may feel that the board individually and collectively is trying to pierce your defenses, seek out your hidden weaknesses and embarrass and confuse you. Actually, this is not true. They are obliged to make an appraisal of your qualifications for the job you are seeking, and they want to see you in your best light. Remember, they must interview all candidates and a non-cooperative candidate may become a failure in spite of their best efforts to bring out his qualifications. Here are 15 suggestions that will help you:

1) Be natural – Keep your attitude confident, not cocky

If you are not confident that you can do the job, do not expect the board to be. Do not apologize for your weaknesses, try to bring out your strong points. The board is interested in a positive, not negative, presentation. Cockiness will antagonize any board member and make him wonder if you are covering up a weakness by a false show of strength.

2) Get comfortable, but don't lounge or sprawl

Sit erectly but not stiffly. A careless posture may lead the board to conclude that you are careless in other things, or at least that you are not impressed by the importance of the occasion. Either conclusion is natural, even if incorrect. Do not fuss with your clothing, a pencil or an ashtray. Your hands may occasionally be useful to emphasize a point; do not let them become a point of distraction.

3) Do not wisecrack or make small talk

This is a serious situation, and your attitude should show that you consider it as such. Further, the time of the board is limited – they do not want to waste it, and neither should you.

4) Do not exaggerate your experience or abilities
In the first place, from information in the application or other interviews and sources, the board may know more about you than you think. Secondly, you probably will not get away with it. An experienced board is rather adept at spotting such a situation, so do not take the chance.

5) If you know a board member, do not make a point of it, yet do not hide it
Certainly you are not fooling him, and probably not the other members of the board. Do not try to take advantage of your acquaintanceship – it will probably do you little good.

6) Do not dominate the interview
Let the board do that. They will give you the clues – do not assume that you have to do all the talking. Realize that the board has a number of questions to ask you, and do not try to take up all the interview time by showing off your extensive knowledge of the answer to the first one.

7) Be attentive
You only have 20 minutes or so, and you should keep your attention at its sharpest throughout. When a member is addressing a problem or question to you, give him your undivided attention. Address your reply principally to him, but do not exclude the other board members.

8) Do not interrupt
A board member may be stating a problem for you to analyze. He will ask you a question when the time comes. Let him state the problem, and wait for the question.

9) Make sure you understand the question
Do not try to answer until you are sure what the question is. If it is not clear, restate it in your own words or ask the board member to clarify it for you. However, do not haggle about minor elements.

10) Reply promptly but not hastily
A common entry on oral board rating sheets is "candidate responded readily," or "candidate hesitated in replies." Respond as promptly and quickly as you can, but do not jump to a hasty, ill-considered answer.

11) Do not be peremptory in your answers
A brief answer is proper – but do not fire your answer back. That is a losing game from your point of view. The board member can probably ask questions much faster than you can answer them.

12) Do not try to create the answer you think the board member wants
He is interested in what kind of mind you have and how it works – not in playing games. Furthermore, he can usually spot this practice and will actually grade you down on it.

13) Do not switch sides in your reply merely to agree with a board member
Frequently, a member will take a contrary position merely to draw you out and to see if you are willing and able to defend your point of view. Do not start a debate, yet do not surrender a good position. If a position is worth taking, it is worth defending.

14) Do not be afraid to admit an error in judgment if you are shown to be wrong

The board knows that you are forced to reply without any opportunity for careful consideration. Your answer may be demonstrably wrong. If so, admit it and get on with the interview.

15) Do not dwell at length on your present job

The opening question may relate to your present assignment. Answer the question but do not go into an extended discussion. You are being examined for a *new* job, not your present one. As a matter of fact, try to phrase ALL your answers in terms of the job for which you are being examined.

Basis of Rating

Probably you will forget most of these "do's" and "don'ts" when you walk into the oral interview room. Even remembering them all will not ensure you a passing grade. Perhaps you did not have the qualifications in the first place. But remembering them will help you to put your best foot forward, without treading on the toes of the board members.

Rumor and popular opinion to the contrary notwithstanding, an oral board wants you to make the best appearance possible. They know you are under pressure – but they also want to see how you respond to it as a guide to what your reaction would be under the pressures of the job you seek. They will be influenced by the degree of poise you display, the personal traits you show and the manner in which you respond.

ABOUT THIS BOOK

This book contains tests divided into Examination Sections. Go through each test, answering every question in the margin. We have also attached a sample answer sheet at the back of the book that can be removed and used. At the end of each test look at the answer key and check your answers. On the ones you got wrong, look at the right answer choice and learn. Do not fill in the answers first. Do not memorize the questions and answers, but understand the answer and principles involved. On your test, the questions will likely be different from the samples. Questions are changed and new ones added. If you understand these past questions you should have success with any changes that arise. Tests may consist of several types of questions. We have additional books on each subject should more study be advisable or necessary for you. Finally, the more you study, the better prepared you will be. This book is intended to be the last thing you study before you walk into the examination room. Prior study of relevant texts is also recommended. NLC publishes some of these in our Fundamental Series. Knowledge and good sense are important factors in passing your exam. Good luck also helps. So now study this Passbook, absorb the material contained within and take that knowledge into the examination. Then do your best to pass that exam.

EXAMINATION SECTION

EXAMINATION SECTION
TEST 1

DIRECTIONS: Each question or incomplete statement is followed by several suggested answers or completions. Select the one that BEST answers the question or completes the statement. *PRINT THE LETTER OF THE CORRECT ANSWER IN THE SPACE AT THE RIGHT.*

1. Counselors on duty during visiting hours at detention centers are required to remain at their posts and to be very watchful until visiting hours are over. During one visiting period, the counselor on duty finds that there are few visitors and that conditions are peaceful in the visiting area.
   Which of the following would be the *most appropriate* behavior for the counselor?

   A. Leave the visiting area to attend to other official duties, but check back frequently to make certain that conditions remain quiet.
   B. Remain in the visiting area and take advantage of untroubled conditions by catching up on needed report writing.
   C. Leave the visiting area to attend to other official duties, but not before arranging for a reliable visitor to summon help immediately if needed.
   D. Remain in the visiting area and pay strict attention to conditions in that area.

   1.____

2. A counselor supervising a group of children in a dormitory in a detention center observes that a newly admitted child appears shy and withdrawn and generally avoids contact with the other children.
   Which of the following would be the BEST action for the counselor to take?

   A. Mentally note the child's behavior and report it to the supervisor if this behavior continues
   B. Advise the child that "the only way to get along is to go along" and that his behavior may cause resentment
   C. Arrange for an older child to initiate the newly arrived child into the group's activities
   D. Ask the child to explain his behavior at the next group counseling session

   2.____

3. A counselor in a dormitory observes two children fighting. Which of the following would be the BEST action for the counselor to take?

   A. Stop the fight quickly
   B. Permit the fight to continue until one child is clearly ahead
   C. Referee the fight to make sure that proper rules are followed
   D. Have one of the stronger children stop the fight

   3.____

4. A counselor in a detention center finds one of the detained children by himself spraying graffiti on his dormitory walls with a spray can.
   Which of the following actions by the counselor is LEAST justified?

   A. Take the spray can away from the child
   B. Have all the children in the dormitory remove the graffiti
   C. Have the child who used the spray can remove the graffiti
   D. Explain to the child who sprayed the walls why he should not have done so

   4.____

5. One of the children in a group asks the counselor for permission to speak to the social worker on an important family matter.
   Which of the following is the BEST action for the counselor to take?

   A. Advise the child to secure the benefits of group counseling before seeing the social worker
   B. Refer the child to the social worker
   C. Interview the child to see if the request is really justified
   D. Explain to the child that self-reliance, and not dependence on the social worker, is the key to maturity

6. One of the responsibilities of a counselor on the night tour of a detention center is to make periodic checks of the children's sleeping quarters and observe any child with unusual sleeping behavior.
   If a counselor has just observed a child with unusual sleeping behavior, what should he do *next*?

   A. Continue his observations on succeeding checks, and, if the behavior is repeated, discuss it with the child
   B. Ignore this behavior if no other children in the sleeping quarters seem to be bothered
   C. Get a fellow staff member to confirm the observation and then wake the child
   D. Report the observed behavior to his superior

7. A counselor in a dormitory has completed a head count of children and finds that the head count is one less than it should be.
   Which of the following is the *next* action the counselor should take?

   A. Immediately report the child missing
   B. Alert the child's nearest relatives and advise them not to shelter a runaway
   C. Check all areas of the dormitory to make certain the child is really missing
   D. Question the other children to learn whether they know the reason for the child's disappearance

8. Al, a sixteen-year-old boy, was described by psychologists as "psychopathic." Ben, another sixteen-year-old boy, was described by psychologists as "inhibited and conformist." Which of the following is MOST correct?

   A. Al is more likely than Ben to become delinquent.
   B. Ben is more likely than Al to become delinquent.
   C. Both boys are about equally likely to become delinquent.
   D. Neither boy is likely to become delinquent.

9. John, one of the juveniles under your supervision, admitted after questioning that he had beaten up Tom, another youth in the institution. John said he did it because Tom is a "punk."
   Of the following, the BEST action to take in response to John's statement would be to

   A. advise John to make certain that someone is a "punk" before taking any action
   B. agree that "punks" deserve to be beaten for the good of the rest of the boys
   C. question John as to why he believes Tom is a "punk" and why "punks" should be beaten
   D. agree reluctantly that Tom is a "punk," but emphasize that he should not have been beaten

10. Children in a juvenile detention center are prohibited from having in their possession items which are unlawful, which will assist them to escape, or which can be used to injure or harm others.
    On the basis of this statement, which of the following items is LEAST likely to be prohibited?

    A. Wire clothes hanger
    B. Door knob with a spindle
    C. Two-foot length of garden hose
    D. Bar of soap

10.____

Questions 11-15.

DIRECTIONS: Answer Questions 11 through 15 *only* on the basis of the information and the sample report form given below.

On the evening of Wednesday, October 30, 2014, a counselor is making a routine check of Dormitory A-3 at Smith Juvenile Center. In checking the bathroom, the counselor discovers that a sink is full of water and is starting to overflow onto the floor. The cold-water tap is leaking and the sink is not draining. The counselor finds a wad of paper blocking the sink drain. When the paper is removed, the sink drains immediately. However, the cold-water tap cannot be turned off. The counselor goes to the desk and begins to fill out the following Repair Request Form. The counselor making the repair request is L. Rolin. The other counselor on duty in Dormitory A-3 is A. Pollitt. The department head for this dormitory is S. Jones.

REPAIR REQUEST FORM
A. Name of Juvenile Center _____
B. Exact location of repair job _____
C. Date _____
D. Type of condition requiring repair _____
_____

E. Signature of staff member requesting repair _____
F. Signature of department head approving _____
G. Signature of repair worker and date repair completed _____
_____ (Date) _____
---

11. The information that should be indicated on Line B of the Repair Request Form is

    A. Smith Juvenile Center   B. Dormitory A
    C. Sink, Smith Juvenile Center D. Bathroom, Dormity A-3

11.____

12. Which of the following is the MOST *exact* and *informative* entry for Line C?

    A. Wednesday evening   B. 2014
    C. October 2011   D. October 30, 2014

12.____

13. Which of the following entries for Line D should be the *most useful* to a repair supervisor in deciding what kind of repair worker should make the repair and what equipment the worker should have?

13.____

- A. Sink was discovered overflowing onto floor
- B. Cold-water tap is leaking
- C. Cold-water tap is dripping and sink is not draining
- D. Sink drain is plugged up

14. The person whose signature should appear on Line E is

   A. L. Rolin
   B. A. Pollitt
   C. S. Jones
   D. the repair worker

15. A line on the Repair Request Form that CANNOT be filled out on the basis of the information given above is

   A. line A   B. line D   C. line F   D. line G

16. Certain youngsters in a juvenile detention facility are constantly fighting with each other. So far no one has been seriously hurt. Another youth who lives in the same dormitory has complained to the counselor because he is afraid he might be involved in future outbreaks, possibly as a victim.
    Of the following, the BEST action for the counselor to take would be to

    A. assure the youth who complained that he really has nothing to fear, because the youngsters complained about fighting only among themselves
    B. explain to the youth who complained that fighting among adolescents is part of the process of "growing up," and that he should be a part of this process if he wants to develop normally
    C. report the matter to his superiors, with a recommendation that the youth who complained should be transferred to another dormitory if possible
    D. watch the situation carefully and take immediate action when someone is seriously hurt

17. A fundamental responsibility of a detention facility is to provide adequate medical care for the juvenile remanded to it. Assume that a youth suddenly complains to a counselor of severe stomach pains.
    Of the following, what is the FIRST action the counselor should take?

    A. Observe the youth for a day to see if the pains persist
    B. Check the youth's medical history to see if he has a pattern of faking illness
    C. Secure medical attention as soon as possible
    D. Try to alleviate the pain with aspirin

18. The gang, like any group, has a powerful influence in enforcing comformity on its members. Individual gang members hate to be considered different from their fellow gang members. For example, the way most members of the gang act or dress is compelling reason for other gang members to do the same.
    Which of the following statements BEST expresses the meaning of the above paragraph?

    A. Gang members live in fear of behaving in a way contrary to gang rules
    B. Force and violence serve to make a gang member conform to the gang way of life
    C. Gang members behave the way they do because society is weak
    D. The behavior of gang members is often governed by their wish to conform

19. Some experts on juvenile groups have observed that, if membership in the delinquent gang were not rewarding to the individual gang member, the gang would cease to exist. The implication of this statement is, *most nearly,* that

    A. the threats of rival gangs serve to unify many delinquent gangs
    B. many gangs are very unstable in membership, and the loyalty of members is low
    C. gang membership meets the needs of some juveniles
    D. the lives of many gang members are characterized by desperation rather than fun

19._____

20. The daytime counselor in a detention center, before going off duty, confers with the incoming nighttime counselor and discusses the behavior of the group during his day tour.
    Of the following, the MAIN reason for this conference should be to

    A. build up a file of experiences useful for group counseling
    B. make the juveniles aware that both counselors are in agreement
    C. alert the oncoming counselor to daytime behavior that may be repeated at night
    D. avoid duplication in written reports of incidents

20._____

Questions 21-25.

DIRECTIONS: Answer Questions 21 through 25 *only* on the basis of the information and the sample form given below.

When children are admitted to a juvenile detention center, all their personal property, including the clothing that they are wearing, is taken away from them. A record is kept of this property on the following Personal Property List and, when they leave the center, all their personal property is returned to them.

SAMPLE FORM FOR LISTING PERSONAL PROPERTY

PERSONAL PROPERTY LIST			
Item	Color	Material	Quantity
Shirt			
Pants			
Belt			
Undershorts			
Undershirt			
Socks			
Sneakers			
Shoes			
Sandals			
Coat			
Hat			
Sweater			
Other (describe)			
Name of Child		Admission Date	

Two children, Allen Adams and Bertram Brown, were admitted to Juvenile Center X on October 1, 2014. An admissions counselor found that they had the following items of personal property:

ALLEN ADAMS - 1 pair white cotton socks, 1 pair blue sneakers, blue cotton shirt, tan wool pants, brown vinyl belt, white cotton under-shorts, white cotton undershirt, wristwatch, brown wool sweater, and a ballpoint pen.

BERTRAM BROWN - 1 pair black cotton socks, 1 pair white sneakers, white polyester shirt, tan cotton pants, white cotton undershorts, white cotton undershirt, tan leather coat, brown plastic wallet with bus pass, and 50¢ in change.

21. Which of the following is the MOST *complete* and *correct* entry for "Shirt" on the Personal Property List for Allen Adams?

    A. White, cotton, one
    B. Blue, wool, one
    C. Blue, cotton, one
    D. White, polyester, one

22. If, at the time of admission, the child does not have with him or is not wearing one of the items listed, the line for that item is left blank.
    Which one of the following items should be left *blank* on the Personal Property List for Bertram Brown?

    A. Pants
    B. Belt
    C. Sneakers
    D. Other

23. Which of the following is the MOST *complete* and *correct* entry for "Other" on the Personal Property List for Allen Adams?

    A. Wristwatch, one; Ballpoint pen, one
    B. Wristwatch, one; Ballpoint pen, one; Sweater, brown, wool, one
    C. Socks, white, cotton, one; Sweater, brown, wool, one
    D. Socks, white, cotton, one; Wristwatch, one; Brown sweater, wool, one

24. For which of the following items should there be NO entry on the Personal Property List either for Allen Adams or for Bertram Brown?

    A. Undershorts
    B. Sneakers
    C. Coat
    D. Hat

25. Allen Adams and Bertram Brown have two items of personal property that are identical in kind, color, and quantity. These *two* items are

    A. Shirt; Pants
    B. Undershorts; Socks
    C. Pants; Undershorts
    D. Undershirt; Undershorts

KEY (CORRECT ANSWERS)

1.	D	11.	D
2.	A	12.	D
3.	A	13.	B
4.	B	14.	A
5.	D	15.	D
6.	C	16.	C
7.	A	17.	C
8.	C	18.	D
9.	C	19.	C
10.	D	20.	C

21. C
22. B
23. A
24. D
25. D

TEST 2

DIRECTIONS: Each question or incomplete statement is followed by several suggested answers or completions. Select the one that BEST answers the question or completes the statement. *PRINT THE LETTER OF THE CORRECT ANSWER IN THE SPACE AT THE RIGHT.*

1. The 14- and 15-year-old youths in male dormitory B have daily group meetings. During one of these meetings, the counselor helps the group to realize that they are being "fooled" and "taken advantage of" by a youth who had achieved a position of leadership in the group as a result of his bullying and his more seriously delinquent behavior. Reducing the group's respect for this youth is

   A. *probably good,* because adolescence is an impressionable period and youths may tend to imitate a more seriously delinquent youth whom they admire
   B. *probably bad,* because a youth involved in more serious delinquency is exactly the kind of experienced leader who can be used to help the counselor keep the other youths "in line"
   C. *probably bad,* because the realization that one of their peers, whom they had trusted, was taking advantage of them will tend to make the youths feel even more anti-social
   D. *probably neither good nor bad,* since young people are not influenced very much by other youths whom they meet in the artificial environment of a detention facility

1.____

2. Of the following, the BEST reason so much research on juvenile delinquency focuses on gangs is that

   A. juvenile delinquency is caused by gangs
   B. the elimination of gangs is very likely to eliminate delinquency among juveniles
   C. individual delinquents very often form gangs or are members of gangs
   D. the highest delinquency rates are found among boys who are aggressive and outgoing

2.____

3. Juvenile delinquency shows many different forms, different degrees of intensity, and varies for many reasons.
   This statement implies, *most nearly,* that

   A. "hard core" delinquents are admired by their peers for stealing or fighting
   B. whether or not a boy is arrested for delinquency depends in part on chance
   C. delinquents should be encouraged to reform their ways
   D. no single cause is sufficient to explain juvenile delinquency

3.____

4. State statutes limit confinement of people under 16 years of age to a maximum of 3 years, regardless of how serious the crime. In practice, relatively few delinquents under 16 are incarcerated in juvenile correction facilities. Of those incarcerated, only a handful are confined more than 15 months, and most are free in less than a year.
   This statement implies that a 14-year-old youth found delinquent by a State Juvenile Court would, *most likely,*

   A. be confined only a few days
   B. be confined only until age 16
   C. be confined for the maximum period of time
   D. not be confined

4.____

5. Juveniles who are remanded to detention facilities often arrive distressed and angry. Some of these juveniles will look upon all counselors, teachers and other members of the detention staff with hostility and distrust.
Of the following, probably the MOST effective way a counselor can communicate genuine concern for the welfare of these detained juveniles is for the counselor to

   A. tell the juveniles frequently that he understands their problems and is concerned about their welfare
   B. appear unconcerned and wait for the juveniles to "test" his concern for them
   C. make an effort to alleviate the problems experienced by juveniles in detention
   D. "play along" with the juveniles by telling them that, although most counselors cannot be trusted, he is different and can be looked upon as a friend

5.____

6. Adolescence is a maturational phase in which the young person is trying to redefine himself. It is a period in which the adolescent is striving to throw off the shackles of childhood and become a person in his own right.
In dealing with the adolescent in a juvenile detention center, which of the following is the BEST approach for a counselor to take?

   A. Be aware that adolescent behavior in general is often inconsistent - mature one moment, immature the next.
   B. Make the detained adolescent aware that he is bad, and that everyone must strictly obey the rules.
   C. Recognize that the youthful offender is basically immature and therefore cannot be held responsible for his actions.
   D. Treat him as an equal and encourage mature behavior by allowing him to make his own interpretations of rules.

6.____

7. During the school year, the children at a juvenile detention center are expected to go to school unless excused by a doctor or for another special reason. One morning a child in a counselor's group refuses to go to school and refuses to explain why.
Of the following, the BEST action for the counselor to take *next* in this situation would be to

   A. escort the child forcibly to the classroom
   B. warn the child of the severe consequences if he persists in his refusal to go
   C. report the matter to his supervisor
   D. permit the child to have his way

7.____

8. Both individual and group counseling are used in juvenile detention centers.
Which of the following is the MOST important reason for the use of group counseling?

   A. It is more efficient for a counselor to share his knowledge with a group all at once than to talk to individuals separately.
   B. Juveniles usually will not respond well to a counselor unless the counselor is part of a group.
   C. The group session is a more direct way for the counselor to observe and deal with group behavior.
   D. Juveniles, who have not yet reached maturity, cannot benefit from individual counseling.

8.____

9. Behavioral problems impair peace and order within the institution and reinforce negative values for the juveniles themselves.
   Which of the following statements about behavior problems in a juvenile detention facility is CORRECT?

   A. Runaways present a problem to group counselors because a group has difficulty in adjusting when one of its members is not present at a session.
   B. Drinking is a problem because it is in violation of a state law which prohibits drinking by persons under 21 years of age.
   C. Sexual problems can be expected to appear in an adolescent population confined in a detention facility.
   D. Behavioral problems do not usually occur among juvenile offenders when counselors have been conscientious in performing their duties.

9._____

10. The counselor must maintain a certain degree of aloofness from the children in the detention center and must maintain his image as a figure of authority.
    Of the following, the BEST approach for the counselor to take in following this concept is to

    A. change rules frequently so as to keep the youths in a state of uncertainty
    B. avoid having the youths obey orders as a personal favor to him because they will then expect favors in return
    C. try to develop as many personal friendships as possible because the youths will not take advantage of a friend
    D. avoid any displays of concern or sympathy for the youths so they will know that the counselor represents society

10._____

Questions 11-17.

DIRECTIONS: Answer Questions 11 through 17 *only* on the basis of the information and the sample report form given below.

S. Perez and W. Carr, counselors in Dormitory C-4 at Robinson Juvenile Center, are on duty in the dormitory on September 17, 2014. At 10:15 A.M., a child suddenly begins screaming in Room 211. W. Carr runs to the room and finds a child, Bobbie Doe, lying on the floor. The child who is screaming is Bobbie Doe's roommate, Leslie Roe. Leslie says that they were both jumping on the beds and Bobbie landed wrong and fell on the floor. Bobbie is moaning now and saying, "I sure landed hard. My head hurts." The counselor sees that there is a slight amount of blood on the back of Bobbie's head, and sends Bobbie to Dr. J. Field in the medical unit to be checked for head injury and other possible injuries. As soon as Bobbie has arrived safely at the medical unit, the counselor fills out the following form.

4 (#2)

```
REPORT OF ACCIDENT TO CHILD
(to be filled out in triplicate)
  1. Name of injured child_____
  2. Date of injury _____  3. Time _____
  4. Describe how injury occurred _____
  5. Signature of counselor _____  6. Date _____
TO BE FILLED IN BY MEDICAL UNIT: _____
  7. Nature of injury  8. Treatment given _____
  9. Further treatment needed _____
  10. Signature of physician or nurse_____ 11. Date _____
```

11. How many copies of the "Report of Accident to Child" is the counselor supposed to make out?   11.____

    A. 1   B. 2   C. 3   D. 4

12. Which of the following names is the CORRECT entry for Item 1 of the report form?   12.____

    A. S. Perez   B. W. Carr   C. Leslie Roe   D. Bobbie Doe

13. Which of the following is the CORRECT entry for Item 2 of the report form?   13.____

    A. 9/17/14   B. 10/17/14   C. 10:15 A.M.   D. 10:15 P.M.

14. An accurate report of the cause of an injury is important for two purposes: First, it gives the medical unit an idea of what kinds of injuries should be looked for; second, it is a record of who or what was responsible for the accident.
    Which one of the following entries for Item 4 BEST fulfills *both* of these purposes?   14.____

    A. Child complained, "My head hurts." Investigation showed some bleeding.
    B. Child was jumping on bed and fell on floor. Child reported that his head was hurt. Head was bleeding slightly.
    C. Child's roommate reported they had been jumping on beds. This behavior is dangerous and it is against the rules.
    D. Child's roommate began screaming when child was hurt. Counselor found child lying on floor and moaning.

15. Which of the following names is the CORRECT entry for Item 5 of the report form?   15.____

    A. S. Perez   B. W. Carr   C. Leslie Roe   D. J. Field

16. Which of the following is the CORRECT entry for Item 6?   16.____

    A. September, A.M., 2014   B. September 2014, 10:15 A.M.
    C. September 17, 2014   D. September 2014, Robinson

17. What information, if any, should the counselor fill in for Item 7?   17.____

    A. "Head injury"
    B. "Injuries from falling on floor"
    C. "Head injury and possible other injuries"
    D. No information

18. Many juvenile detention facilities focus on vocational training, rather than academic training, for children of high school age.
    Of the following, the BEST reason for emphasizing vocational training is that

    A. most juveniles in a detention facility have a lower than average IQ and frequently are not able to do academic high school work
    B. detained juveniles of high school age usually benefit more from job training
    C. a high school diploma cannot be awarded in the state to a person under legal detention
    D. qualified teachers of academic subjects are in short supply and their higher salaries would be a drain on the detention center's budget

18.____

19. During a visiting period between parents and children in a juvenile detention center, a heated argument between a parent and his child is observed by the counselor on duty. The counselor succeeds in stopping the argument but not in solving the problem that led to the argument.
    Which of the following would be the BEST action for the counselor to take next?

    A. Continue his efforts to solve the problem on the parent's next visit
    B. Report the incident and the problem to his supervisor
    C. Admonish the child after the visit and explain that arguing with parents is unacceptable behavior
    D. Advise the parent that he should refrain from further visits until he can stop verbally abusing his child

19.____

Questions 20-22.

DIRECTIONS: Answer Questions 20 through 22 on the basis of the information and the list below.

The following list gives dates on which 8 children were admitted to a juvenile detention center:

Name	Admission Date
Abner, E	November 6, 2014
Alvarez, L.	October 24, 2014
Blake, G.	October 31, 2014
Charlton, M.	November 7, 2014
Davis, A.	November 8, 2014
Green, M.	November 1, 2014
Figua, J.	October 31, 2014
Smith, O.	October 25, 2014

20. The children who have been at the center for less than one week as of November 12, 2014, are:

    A. Alvarez, L.; Blake, G.; Figua, J.
    B. Abner, E.; Charlton, M.; Davis, A.
    C. Charlton, M.; Davis, A.; Green, M.
    D. Davis, A.; Green, M.; Figua, J.

20.____

21. The children who have been at the center for at least one week but less than two weeks as of November 12, 2014, are:

    A. Blake, G.; Green, M.; Figua, J.
    B. Charlton, M.; Davis, A.; Smith, O.
    C. Alvarez, L.; Blake, G.; Figua, J.
    D. Blake, G.; Figua, J.; Smith, O.

22. The children who have been at the center for at least two weeks but less than three weeks as of November 12, 2014, are:

    A. Alvarez, L.; Smith, O.
    B. Alvarez, L.; Blake, G.; Green, M.; Figua, J.
    C. Charlton, M.; Davis, A.
    D. Alvarez, L.; Blake, G.; Figua, J.

23. A child in a juvenile detention center dormitory signs a sick call sheet and asks to see a doctor. The counselor on duty in the dormitory suspects that the child is not really sick but wants attention.
    Which of the following would be the BEST action for the counselor to take?

    A. Remove the child's name from the sick call sheet and arrange for the child to be a leader in the next round of group activities
    B. Remove the child's name from the sick call sheet and explain to the child that making a fuss over trivial matters is not the way to become noticed
    C. Allow the child to be examined by the doctor and make no comment to the child about the suspicion that he is not sick
    D. Allow the child to be examined by the doctor but tell the child that faking will not be tolerated in the future

24. A counselor supervising a visiting area in a detention center is also acting as a representative of the center. The visiting public's impression of the center depends partly on the counselor's behavior.
    Which of the following would be the *most appropriate* behavior for a counselor supervising a visiting area?

    A. Urge the visitors to help rehabilitate the children
    B. Advise the children to avoid visitors who seem to have problems
    C. Apologize to the visitors for the state statutes on juvenile justice
    D. Watch the visiting area carefully and treat all present politely

25. Deviants are labeled as such by those with the power and prestige to establish the rules of society as a whole; individuals who seriously defy these rules are considered deviants. However, deviants often reject society's negative labels and endeavor to use their subculture as a base to acquire power and prestige in the general society. If successful, their former deviancy may come to be regarded by society generally as a normal variation of behavior. This statement means, *most nearly,* that

    A. power plays an important role in society's definition of deviancy
    B. power and prestige are not sought by deviants
    C. deviants who reject society's negative labels acquire power
    D. power is acquired by defying society's rules

KEY (CORRECT ANSWERS)

1.	A	11.	C
2.	C	12.	D
3.	D	13.	A
4.	D	14.	B
5.	C	15.	B
6.	A	16.	C
7.	C	17.	D
8.	C	18.	B
9.	C	19.	B
10.	B	20.	B

21. A
22. A
23. C
24. D
25. A

TEST 3

DIRECTIONS: Each question or incomplete statement is followed by several suggested answers or completions. Select the one that BEST answers the question or completes the statement. *PRINT THE LETTER OF THE CORRECT ANSWER IN THE SPACE AT THE RIGHT.*

1. A child in a juvenile detention center tells his counselor that he is very worried about problems at home and the ability of his parents to cope with these problems. Which of the following would be the BEST action for the counselor to take?   1.____

    A. Impress upon the child the fact that if he had not misbehaved he would be home helping his parents
    B. Report the child's concern to the center's social worker
    C. Explain to the child that excessive concern about parents and their problems may damage his normal development
    D. Instruct the child to avoid the fate of his parents through discipline and self-improvement

2. Some experts believe that much delinquency is not really deeply rooted, but is an immediate response to an immediate situation.   2.____
Which of the following is the BEST example of a solution to the type of situation described in the preceding quotation?

    A. Improved recreation programs for youth in slums
    B. Special rehabilitative efforts for aggressive delinquents
    C. Special anti-theft devices installed on automobiles
    D. Improved school counseling programs for slow learners

Questions 3-9.

DIRECTIONS: Answer Questions 3 through 9 *only* on the basis of the information in the passage below.

Laws concerning juveniles make it clear that the function of the courts is to treat delinquents, not to punish them. Many years ago, children were detained in jails or police lockups along with adult offenders. Today, however, it is recognized that separate detention is important for the protection of the children. Detention is now regarded as part of the treatment process.

Detention is not an ordinary child care job. On the one hand, it must be distinguished from mere shelter care, which is a custodial program for children whose families cannot care for them adequately. On the other hand, it must be distinguished from treatment in mental health institutions, which is meant for children who have very serious mental or psychological problems. The children in a detention facility are there because they have run into trouble with the law, and because they must be kept in safe custody for a short period until the court decides the final action to be taken in each child's case.

The Advisory Committee on Detention and Shelter Care has outlined several basic objectives for a good detention service. One objective is secure custody. Like adults who are being detained until their cases come up before the court, children too will often want to escape from detention. Security measures must be adequate to prevent ordinary escape attempts, although at the same time a jail-like atmosphere should be avoided. Another objective is to provide constructive activities for the children and to give individual guidance through casework and group sessions. A final objective is to study each child individually so that useful information can be provided for court action and so that the mental, emotional, or other problems that have contributed to the child's difficulties can be identified.

3. According to the above passage, laws concerning juveniles make it clear that the *main* aim of the courts in handling young offenders is to

   A. punish juvenile delinquents
   B. provide treatment for juvenile delinquents
   C. relieve the families of juvenile delinquents
   D. counsel families which have juvenile delinquents

4. The passage *implies* that the former practice of locking up juveniles along with adults was

   A. *good*, because it was more efficient than providing separate facilities
   B. *good*, because children could then be protected by the adults
   C. *bad*, because the children were not safe
   D. *bad*, because delinquents need mental health treatment

5. The passage says that a detention center differs from a shelter care facility in that the children in a detention center

   A. have been placed there permanently by their families or by the courts
   B. come from families who cannot or will not care for them
   C. have serious mental or psychological problems
   D. are in trouble with the law and must be kept in safe custody temporarily

6. The passage mentions one specific way in which detained juveniles are like detained adults. This similarity is that both detained juveniles and detained adults

   A. may try to escape from the detention facility
   B. have been convicted of serious crimes
   C. usually come from bad family backgrounds
   D. have mental or emotional problems

7. The passage lists several basic objectives that were out-lined by the Advisory Committee on Detention and Child Care. Which one of the following aims is NOT given in the list of Advisory Committee objectives?

   A. Separating juvenile offenders from adult offenders
   B. Providing secure custody
   C. Giving individual guidance
   D. Providing useful information for court action

8. The passage mentions a "custodial program." This means, *most nearly*,

   A. janitor services
   B. a program to prevent jail escapes
   C. caretaking services for dependent children
   D. welfare payments to families with children

9. The passage says that "security measures" are needed in a detention center PRIMARILY in order to

    A. prevent unauthorized persons from entering
    B. prevent juveniles from escaping
    C. ensure that records are safeguarded for court action
    D. create a jail-like atmosphere

10. Juveniles at a detention center are permitted to smoke cigarettes during smoking periods if they are over fourteen and have the written consent of their parents. A juvenile over fourteen, but without parental written consent, repeatedly asks a counselor for a cigarette during a smoking period.
    Which of the following would be the BEST action for the counselor to take?

    A. Tell the juvenile to get a cigarette from another child but to make sure that the counselor does not see him smoking
    B. Give the juvenile a cigarette if, in the counselor's opinion, it would help the juvenile's adjustment to the center
    C. Explain to the juvenile that he will be permitted to smoke when he secures his parents' consent
    D. Urge the juvenile to display maturity and not bother the counselor with trivial requests

11. Children newly admitted to a juvenile detention center are first assigned to the reception center dormitory where a daytime counselor explains the rules and regulations of the center.
    Which of the following would be the BEST way for the counselor to insure that the children understand these rules? Explain

    A. *thoroughly* but do not allow questions by the children, because too many questions would tend to confuse them
    B. *briefly,* but give a short written quiz to the children right afterward, giving a more thorough explanation to those who fail
    C. *thoroughly* and advise the children to save any questions for practical situations as they arise during their stay at the detention center
    D. *thoroughly* and allow a question and answer period at the end

12. A counselor in a detention center confiscates the contraband he has found in a child's possession.
    Which of the following is the BEST action for the counselor to take *next*?

    A. Report the incident to his superior
    B. Inform the child that serious consequences will follow any future incidents of this nature
    C. Turn the contraband over to the nearest police precinct
    D. Arrange for the contraband's burning at the borough sanitation incinerator

13. The family is a vital component in any program of juvenile delinquency prevention and treatment.
    Which of the following would probably contribute LEAST to making families function better?

A. Better housing for the family
B. More restrictive legislation regarding divorce and adultery
C. Increased employment opportunities for members of the family
D. Expanded family planning education

14. When a social worker tells the counselor that a child is "culturally deprived," the counselor is *most likely* to find that the child

   A. is illegitimate
   B. comes from a broken home
   C. is a "slow learner" and might be slightly retarded
   D. has not had as much opportunity or motivation as most children to develop academic skills

15. Recreational programs are important in the success of a rehabilitation program. Of the following, the BEST method for the counselor to use to insure that the time allotted for recreation achieves the greatest possible success in rehabilitation would be to

   A. specialize in one or two competitive sports so that a youth will have sufficient practice to win and experience the accomplishment of victory over his peers
   B. keep the recreation time quiet, because, if adolescents get excited and worked up during a play session, they will be behavior problems for the rest of the day
   C. include non-competitive activities in addition to the usual athletic competition since many of the detained youths have never successfully competed anywhere
   D. make it clear that recreation time is a reward for good behavior and can be withheld as a punishment

16. Many family research experts believe that the relationship between parent and child in this country has a great influence on the personality and development of the child. Which of the following statements BEST represents the opinion of most of these experts concerning parental influence in the child's personality development?

   A. Mothers and fathers have approximately equal impact on their children, regardless of the age or sex of the child.
   B. Fathers have very little impact on their children until the child is 16, after which they have approximately equal impact with the mother.
   C. Mothers and fathers tend to have different effects on their children, depending partly on the age and sex of both parent and child.
   D. The mother's influence on the child, regardless of the sex of the child, is overwhelming up to the age of six, after which the father's influence is predominant, regardless of the sex of the child.

17. A growing child needs group activity in order to develop socially. A gang is one example of such a group. Joining a gang often answers a boy's needs for companionship and adventure. He gets the feeling of belonging and of loyalty to the group. If the gang is delinquent, the tougher the boy is, the more recognition he gets from the gang. He may also find the discipline he needs because gangs frequently develop their own codes and rules of behavior and demand that their members rigidly abide by them.
On the basis of the foregoing statement, if a child joins a gang, which of the following is *most probably* TRUE?

   A. He will become an adult criminal.
   B. He could not find enough companionship and sense of belonging outside the gang.

C. The gang was formed to commit acts of violence.
D. He has been in a detention facility several times already.

18. There are many theories of the causes of delinquent behavior. One approach sees delinquent behavior as the normal response of many adolescents to conditions of social and economic deprivation characteristic of the lower class. This statement *implies* that 18.____

A. delinquent behavior is a neurotic response to repeated personal failure
B. the root of the delinquency problem is to be found in destructive family relationships
C. delinquency is more related to a particular kind of social environment than it is to individual character
D. delinquent behavior can be treated by modifying individual patterns of personal feeling, behavior, and relationships

KEYS (CORRECT ANSWERS)

1. B
2. C
3. B
4. C
5. D

6. A
7. A
8. C
9. B
10. C

11. D
12. A
13. B
14. D
15. C

16. C
17. B
18. C

EXAMINATION SECTION
TEST 1

DIRECTIONS: Each question or incomplete statement is followed by several suggested answers or completions. Select the one that BEST answers the question or completes the statement. *PRINT THE LETTER OF THE CORRECT ANSWER IN THE SPACE AT THE RIGHT.*

1. During the first few days in a children's institution, some children will keep to themselves, refuse to take part in activities, and even refuse to eat.
   To help counselors deal effectively with such behavior, the supervisor should point out that these children are PROBABLY

   A. stubborn and they should be forced to take part in the activities
   B. behaving this way because they dislike their counselor
   C. feeling inferior, lonely, unwanted, and depressed
   D. showing signs of serious emotional disturbance

   1.____

2. Most children between the ages of six and eight are eager to show adults that they can do things for themselves such as getting their food, dressing, and taking care of their personal hygiene, and are apt to resent being *helped* or *watched* by adults.
   However, of the following, it is MOST important for child-care workers to realize that children

   A. will mature emotionally only if they are strictly supervised
   B. also want and need adults to be concerned about them
   C. should be told that they cannot be independent
   D. should be taught not to resent constant supervision by adults

   2.____

3. Assume a supervisor has learned that one of his subordinates punished a child he caught in the bathroom alone, masturbating.
   Of the following, the MOST appropriate action for the supervisor to take is to

   A. praise the subordinate for his action
   B. suggest that the child be given psychological consultation
   C. discuss with the subordinate his attitude about masturbation and the need to respect the child's privacy
   D. speak with the child privately and tell him he may be endangering his health

   3.____

4. A counselor asks the supervisor for advice about a seven-year-old boy who is often found with matches in his possession.
   The BEST suggestion the supervisor can make is that the counselor should FIRST

   A. find out whether the boy is smoking cigarettes
   B. watch the boy closely to find out what he is doing with the matches
   C. try to discover what psychological meaning the matches have for this boy
   D. tell the boy firmly about the danger of fire and take the matches away

   4.____

5. A thirteen-year-old boy who has committed thefts and was adjudged to be neglected is placed in a shelter.
   His *initial* attitude towards his counselor is MOST likely to be

   5.____

A. ambivalent
B. aggressively friendly
C. hostile and rejecting
D. sympathetic

6. If a counselor has a child in his group who stutters badly, finds it difficult to talk with the other children in his group, and is withdrawing into himself, he can *probably* BEST help the child by

    A. telling him that he will stop stuttering if he speaks slowly
    B. taking him aside as frequently as possible and giving him speech exercises
    C. stopping him every time he begins to stutter
    D. asking the other children to cooperate by not calling attention to the stuttering

7. A counselor complains frequently to the supervisor that the eight- to ten-year-old boys in his dormitory are not quiet at any time and are always creating disturbances. Of the following, the BEST suggestion the supervisor can make to the counselor is to

    A. examine carefully his relationships with the children
    B. give the children more things to do that interest them
    C. let the children know that many other youngsters find it hard to be quiet
    D. teach them the value of patience and the importance of learning to be quiet

8. Some eight- and nine-year-old children at the shelter refuse to take part in active outdoor sports, preferring to play quietly.
Assuming that these children have no physical or mental disability, the counselor should realize that

    A. children's choice of activities often depends on their experiences and skills
    B. when children are angry because they are placed in the institution, they show their anger by refusing to participate in group sports
    C. this behavior indicates emotional disturbance and requires psychiatric consultation
    D. organized games or group play are difficult for most children at this age

9. A ten-year-old boy seems to have difficulty reading any of the children's books that are available at the shelter. Of the following, the BEST recommendation that could be made in this situation is that

    A. books be found that will interest the child
    B. the child be told that reading is hard work
    C. the child be transferred to a younger age group
    D. the child be tested for reading ability

10. Counselors will often turn to the supervisor for on-the-spot solutions to problems that they have been unable to work out. Assume that a counselor has asked his supervisor what he should do when a 10-year-old child repeatedly asks for help in tying his shoelaces. The child does not seem to know how to begin.
It would be MOST appropriate for the supervisor to tell the counselor

    A. to patiently attempt to teach the child how to tie his shoelaces
    B. that the child is probably pretending that he does not know how to tie his laces in order to get special attention
    C. to recommend psychological consultation in the interest of the child
    D. that he should insist that the child learn to lace his own shoes

11. Susie, an eight-year-old, becomes terribly upset, abusive, and destructive when urged to eat certain foods that she has never eaten before.
The BEST way for her counselor to help Susie is by

    A. insisting that she eat everything, for the benefit of her health
    B. rewarding her in little ways if she eats these foods
    C. ignoring her outbursts, since this will force her to eat
    D. accepting the fact that many children have a valid dislike for unfamiliar foods

11.____

12. Assume that a twelve-year-old boy, just admitted to the shelter, refuses to undress or even to take off his sweater.
Of the following, the BEST thing for the counselor to do would be to

    A. talk with the boy about his reasons without pressuring him
    B. establish authority immediately by forcing the boy to undress
    C. punish the boy by taking away privileges until he conforms
    D. shame the boy by telling him he is acting like a baby

12.____

13. Assume that a supervisor has evidence that a children's counselor has brought marijuana and other drugs into the institution.
The supervisor's FIRST action should be to

    A. report the situation to the director immediately
    B. warn the counselor that he will be discharged if he is found with drugs
    C. determine whether the counselor has introduced the children to drugs
    D. make a complete investigation and report his findings to the director

13.____

14. The CHIEF cause of death among people between 15 and 25 years of age is

    A. lead poisoning   B. drug abuse
    C. suicide   D. malnutrition

14.____

15. Recent studies show that there has been a trend toward an overall decline in the number of children cared for in institutions.
The MOST important reason for this *decline* is that

    A. fewer children are adjudged to be neglected
    B. funds are lacking to provide institutional care in accordance with approved standards
    C. there is a shortage of qualified personnel to operate the institutions
    D. there is an increased life span of parents

15.____

16. Of the following, the MOST important role played by the mother in the healthy development of a young girl is to

    A. teach her to cook and clean
    B. protect her from immoral influences
    C. provide a female figure with whom she can identify
    D. encourage her to become popular with boys

16.____

17. The one of the following which is the MOST important factor in the present trend toward a lower birth rate in this country is the

    A. new morality   B. high cost of living
    C. women's liberation movement D. new abortion laws

17.____

18. Within the last few years, there has been a reorganization of public human service agencies in the city.
    The Department of Social Services is now part of the

    A. Environmental Protection Administration
    B. Health Services Administration
    C. Board of Education
    D. Human Resources Administration

19. The agency that works mainly with the public school children who are having school adjustment problems is the

    A. Pupils' Placement Division
    B. Department of Mental Hygiene
    C. Department of Social Services
    D. Bureau of Child Guidance

20. The agency that has LEGAL authority to protect children frori mistreatment by adults is the

    A. S.P.C.C.   B. B.P.C.J.   C. S.P.C.A.   D. J.B.G.

21. An organization whose SOLE purpose is to help fatherless boys is the

    A. Angel Guardian Society
    B. Police Athletic League
    C. Sandlot Baseball Association
    D. Big Brothers

22. It is estimated that about one-fifth of the children in the United States live in families with poverty-level incomes.
    The Federal Office of Economic Opportunity has established that a family of four is living in poverty if its income is *at or below*

    A. $10,800   B. $13,500   C. $18,000   D. $25,0.00

23. The one of the following that has recently gained widespread attention for its work to improve conditions for the poor in this country is the

    A. Social Security Administration
    B. Citizens' Committee for Children
    C. National Welfare Rights Organization
    D. Institute for Social Progress

24. The office of probation is doing away with the detention of adolescent offenders in security (locked-door) facilities MAINLY because this method

    A. is no longer needed since these offenders may now be let out on bail
    B. is no longer needed, due to the greater availability of foster homes for adolescents
    C. was often misused, and adolescents were mistreated instead of being educated or rehabilitated
    D. did not provide for any educational facilities

25. A counselor on the night shift reports that there has been an unusual amount of bedwetting in the intermediate boys' dormitory during the past two weeks. He has tried everything and now he thinks that they are doing it *just to be mean* to him. He names two or three boys who have probably put the others up to it.
Of the following, the MOST helpful action for the supervisor to take FIRST would be to

   A. find out whether anything upsetting happened to the boys in the previous two weeks
   B. meet with all the bedwetters in a group and tell them they will be punished if they wet their beds again
   C. question some of the boys to see whether the counselor correctly identified the leaders
   D. advise the night counselor to be more patient

25.____

KEY (CORRECT ANSWERS)

1.	C	11.	D
2.	B	12.	A
3.	C	13.	A
4.	D	14.	B
5.	C	15.	D
6.	D	16.	C
7.	B	17.	D
8.	A	18.	D
9.	D	19.	D
10.	C	20.	A

21. D
22. C
23. C
24. C
25. A

TEST 2

DIRECTIONS: Each question or incomplete statement is followed by several suggested answers or completions. Select the one that BEST answers the question or completes the statement. *PRINT THE LETTER OF THE CORRECT ANSWER IN THE SPACE AT THE RIGHT.*

1. Many children in institutions feel such great resentment about their situation that they are angry at everybody and become disrespectful to counselors.
   The BEST way for supervisors to help counselors deal with this problem is to

   A. advise the counselors to mimic the children's angry responses in order to show them how difficult they are to live with
   B. take every opportunity to show the counselors what they have done wrong in handling these children
   C. discuss with the counselors the causes of the children's resentment and the importance of not reacting impulsively to their misbehavior
   D. provide the counselors with a reading list of books and articles on child development

1.____

2. Assume that a usually quiet, rather obese boy started a fistfight when another boy teased him for being fat.
   Of the following, it would be BEST for the counselor to

   A. tell the boy who started the fight that he would not be teased if he lost weight
   B. help the boys settle the matter and warn them that they will be disciplined if they fight again
   C. punish both the fat boy and the boy who teased him
   D. punish the boy who started the fight

2.____

3. A counselor comes to a supervisor asking for advice about a child that he frequently has to remind to be less noisy during the periods when the children are resting. The child temporarily quiets down when told to do so, but the counselor has become concerned about how to handle the situation.
   The supervisor should advise the counselor that his BEST approach would be to

   A. warn the child that he will be moved to another dormitory if he continues to be noisy
   B. find out if the other children are disturbed by this child before taking stronger disciplinary measures
   C. segregate him from the other children at rest periods and let him be as noisy as he pleases
   D. take away television privileges until the child improves

3.____

4. The one of the following that would be a POOR way for a counselor to deal with tough and unfriendly teenagers is to

   A. suggest that they tell him when they think he fails to maintain the standards he demands of them
   B. resist their attempts to make him explain the reasons for new rules
   C. refrain from talking down to them
   D. encourage them to ask for an explanation whenever they do not understand something

4.____

5. Assume that a child has just swallowed some turpentine that was accidentally left within his reach.
   Which of the following is NOT a recommended measure in giving first aid to the child before the doctor arrives?

   A. Keep the child warm
   B. Induce vomiting
   C. Give hot coffee or tea
   D. Give mineral oil

6. Some professionals, such as psychiatrists, psychologists, teachers, and social workers, have a low opinion of the child-care worker's job and his value to the children.
   Of the following, the MOST serious consequence of such an attitude is that it may

   A. affect the children and their feeling of respect for their counselors
   B. discourage child-care workers from getting more education and professional training
   C. increase the children's hostility toward professionals on the institution's staff
   D. cause child-care workers to resent their supervisor as well as the professionals

7. Assume that one of the boys becomes uncontrollable during the pottery-making periods on the weekly schedule, throwing materials around, upsetting equipment, annoying the other children, and refusing to work on any suggested projects. This does not occur at any other time. This boy's counselor tells his supervisor that he does not know how to handle this situation.
   The supervisor should suggest that the boy

   A. be excluded from recreational activities
   B. be put in another pottery group with a different counselor
   C. be given an activity that he prefers during this period
   D. has fears about getting his hands dirty

8. A child tells a counselor that she does not wish to go on a picnic with her group, even though she has always gone willingly on such outings in the past. When urged to go, she becomes upset and says she is too tired.
   The MOST advisable action for the counselor to take FIRST is to

   A. tell the child that she will have to stay in the infirmary if she is too tired to go on the picnic
   B. tell the child that she has to go because all the arrangements have been made
   C. tell the child that she will lose other privileges if she does not go on the picnic
   D. try to determine the child's real reason for not wanting to go on this trip

9. A 14-year-old boy is found with a knife, refuses to give it up, and threatens to *use it* on the counselor. Of the following, the BEST action for the counselor to take would be to

   A. order the boy to go to the director's office
   B. ignore the matter so that the other boys will not become involved
   C. tell the boy you will take this up with him later
   D. call the supervisor for assistance in handling the matter

10. A counselor seeks advice from the supervisor about a child who has refused for the third time to help tidy up the dormitory.
    Of the following, the BEST suggestion for the supervisor to make would be that the counselor should

A. have punished the child the first time he refused to help
B. pay no attention to this incident
C. ask the child whether he needs or wants help and also try to find out why he refused
D. try to *shame* the child in front of the other children for being lazy

11. A seven-year-old boy runs away from his group while on an outing, but is soon returned to the shelter by the police. This is the first time the boy has run away, and he has otherwise made a good adjustment at the shelter.
The MOST appropriate action for the counselor to take is to

    A. ask the other children to help keep an eye on him during future outings
    B. take away the boy's privileges until he *learns his lesson*
    C. ask the boy whether he wants to transfer to another group
    D. welcome the boy back and try to find out why he ran away and what happened

12. When a child in an institution is afraid or confused, the MOST appropriate action for his counselor to take FIRST is to

    A. recommend that he play with younger children
    B. consider psychiatric referral
    C. insist that he follow the daily routines without deviation
    D. give him sincere individual attention

13. Children in institutions often lie when they are questioned by adults.
The BEST way for counselors to approach this problem is to

    A. make these children aware that adults know they often lie
    B. promise the children that they will not be punished if they tell the truth
    C. listen objectively to the children's statements without assuming they are lying
    D. point out to the children that lying usually results in punishment

14. When a teenager is in trouble, the immediate reaction of many adults is to be unsympathetic and to *teach him* a *lesson*.
The BEST approach for a counselor to take FIRST with a teenage boy who feels that he has been treated unfairly by a recreation worker who has put him out of the gym for alleged misconduct is to

    A. ignore the boy's complaints and begin talking about something else
    B. listen to the boy's side of the story
    C. tell the boy he must learn not to question a person in authority
    D. quietly tell the boy to keep away from the recreation worker after this

15. Frequently a child who comes to a shelter says that he was sent away from his family because he was bad and his parents did not want him any more.
The BEST way for the counselor to begin to help such a child is to

    A. show his understanding of the child's feelings about leaving home and welcome him warmly
    B. tell him that he will be loved at the shelter if his behavior is good
    C. make him realize he was not bad by asking him to give you examples of his good behavior
    D. tell him that the social worker will explain to his family that he is not bad

16. The one of the following relating to young children which has received MOST attention from citizens and professional groups recently is

    A. the recurrence of poliomyelitis
    B. allowances for school lunches
    C. day care programs
    D. rubella immunization

17. The MAIN reason for transferring children from shelters to other institutions or foster homes is to provide

    A. another chance for the children to adjust
    B. a more permanent and stable living arrangement for the children
    C. a more economical method of caring for the children
    D. a structured environment for the children

18. Of the following, the experience that is LEAST likely to be a condition resulting in placement of a six-year-old child in a shelter maintained by the Department of Social Services is

    A. having little food in the house
    B. being threatened with a gun or a knife by a parent
    C. wandering away from home to an unfamiliar neighborhood
    D. being physically abused by a parent

19. When a child is remanded to the shelter by the court, the child's legal status is that his

    A. legal guardian is an appointee of the Commissioner of Social Service
    B. legal guardian is the court
    C. legal guardian is the superintendent of the shelter
    D. guardian is his parent

20. Assume that a child complains to a counselor of not feeling well. The counselor immediately tells the child to go to the nurse. When the child lingers, the counselor pushes him gently, but firmly, towards the nurse's station.
    Of the following, the BEST appraisal of this situation is that the counselor

    A. should have explored the child's complaint further, and accompanied him to the nurse
    B. was right in not exploring the child's complaint, since he has had no medical training
    C. need not have pushed the child, since his lingering showed he probably did not require medical attention
    D. was probably outsmarted by the child who was pretending he was ill

21. As the supervisor on your floor, you have noticed that several of the counselors speak to the children mainly in order to correct them for minor infractions.
    The BEST way to approach this situation is to

    A. tell the counselors that what they are doing is wrong, and order them to stop immediately
    B. explain to these counselors that the children need warmth and friendliness more than correction about minor matters

C. agree that most children do not pay attention if you speak kindly to them
D. suggest that the counselors appoint child monitors to correct the others

22. Assume that several counselors at a children's shelter have complained to one of the supervisors that the daily program schedules are too confining for the children and do not give the counselors enough freedom of action. The counselors want the schedules abolished.
It would be BEST for the supervisor to

    A. recommend that the counselors talk to the director about this matter
    B. help the counselors understand that the organization of time is important for these children as it helps to create order in their lives
    C. tell the counselors that schedules are the best method of keeping children out of trouble
    D. suggest that each counselor turn in his own schedule for approval

23. A supervisor overhears a group of children saying that they have to be pretty careful about what they do or say around their counselor because they *do not want to be slapped*.
The MOST appropriate action for the supervisor to take FIRST is to

    A. warn the counselor that he can be dismissed for slapping children
    B. report the situation to the director of the institution
    C. observe the counselor more closely and attempt to get the facts of the situation
    D. report the counselor to the Child Protective Unit on charges of child abuse

24. The one of the following which is an IMPORTANT reason why counselors should not strike children under any circumstances is that

    A. children may learn that violence is the only way to settle their differences with others
    B. older children are likely to strike the counselors in return
    C. they may injure the children so seriously that parents will prosecute them for child abuse
    D. strict laws against corporal punishment by teachers and counselors have recently been put into effect

25. A supervisor overhears a counselor telling a child that he will not be allowed to skip his evening shower, although the child took a shower earlier after swimming. The supervisor should tell the counselor later that his refusal to make an exception in this case was

    A. *incorrect*, because the second shower is wasting the child's time
    B. *correct*, because the other children would think the counselor is playing favorites and, therefore, lose their respect for him
    C. *incorrect*, because a counselor should consider individual needs whenever possible
    D. correct, because control will be lost when exceptions to rules are tolerated

KEY (CORRECT ANSWERS)

1. C
2. B
3. B
4. B
5. B

6. A
7. C
8. D
9. D
10. C

11. D
12. D
13. C
14. B
15. A

16. C
17. B
18. C
19. D
20. A

21. B
22. B
23. C
24. A
25. C

EXAMINATION SECTION
TEST 1

DIRECTIONS: Each question or incomplete statement is followed by several suggested answers or completions. Select the one that BEST answers the question or completes the statement. *PRINT THE LETTER OF THE CORRECT ANSWER IN THE SPACE AT THE RIGHT.*

1. Which one of the following "suggestions to interviewers" should be AVOIDED?

    A. Encourage the client to verbalize his thoughts and feelings.
    B. Cover as much as possible in each interview.
    C. Don't hesitate to refer the client to someone else who might be more helpful in the situation.
    D. The problem which is presented initially, or the one which seems most obvious, often is not the real one.

2. If it seems clear that disturbance in parents' marital relationships is a major factor in causing a child to be emotionally disturbed, the counselor should

    A. point this out to the parents and tell them that for the welfare of their children, they should resolve their difficulties
    B. suggest that he will be willing to discuss their marital difficulties with them
    C. ignore this and concentrate on helping the child
    D. tactfully suggest that their marital difficulties may be playing a part in their child's disturbance and offer to refer the parents to a qualified marriage counseling service

3. The process of collecting, analyzing, synthesizing and interpreting information about the client should be

    A. completed prior to counseling
    B. completed early in the counseling process
    C. limited to counseling which is primarily diagnostic in purpose
    D. continuous throughout counseling

4. Catharsis, the "emotional unloading" of the client's feelings, has a value in the early stages of counseling because it accomplishes all BUT which one of the following goals?

    A. It relieves strong physiological tensions in the client.
    B. It increases the client's anxiety and therefore his motivation to continue counseling.
    C. It provides a verbal substitute for "acting out" the client's aggressive feelings.
    D. It releases emotional energy which the client has been using to maintain his defenses.

5. During the first interview, the counselor can expect the client to participate at his BEST when the counselor

    A. structures the nature of the counseling process
    B. attempts to summarize the client's problem for him
    C. allows the client to verbalize at his own pace
    D. tells the client that he understands the presenting problem

6. To obtain the most effective results in change of attitude and behavior through parent education, the leader should be

   A. thoroughly grounded in the whole field of psychology
   B. able to help members of the group look at their own attitudes and behavior in constructive ways
   C. completely confident as to the right solution to problems that may be brought up
   D. a warm, charming, friendly human being

7. A social worker's report about a client states that a mother has ambivalent feelings concerning her child. This means that the mother

   A. has contradictory emotional reactions concerning her child
   B. is overprotective of the child
   C. strongly rejects the child
   D. is unduly apprehensive about the child's welfare

8. A psychological report notes, "The client shows little effect." This means that the client

   A. did not take the test too seriously
   B. did not show emotional behavior in situations which normally call for such reactions
   C. did not show signs of fatigue as the testing progressed
   D. reacted to the test situation in a generally favorable manner

9. A psychologist's report states, in part, that a client exhibits some masochistic symptoms. This will be evident to the counselor through the client's persistent attempts at

   A. self-assertion
   B. self-effacement
   C. inflicting physical harm on others
   D. sexual molestation of others of the same sex

10. According to research studies, the type of counselor response that is MOST often followed by a client's expression of insight or illumination is

    A. clarification of feeling
    B. reflection of feeling
    C. simple acceptance
    D. exploratory question

11. Of the following, the BEST way to deal with a 12-year-old boy who feels inferior to his peers is to

    A. provide tasks which he can master with little difficulty
    B. show him how irrational his feelings are
    C. accept his declarations of lack of confidence sympathetically
    D. carefully arrange situations in which he will be obliged to show leadership

12. In counseling or psychotherapy, the factor which is the MOST important for success tends to be the

    A. counselor's theoretical orientation
    B. counselor's attitudes and feelings toward the client

C. techniques used by the counselor
D. amount of experience and training possessed by the counselor

13. Transference is an important aspect of   13.____

    A. test construction   B. grade placement
    C. anecdotal record keeping D. therapy

14. The MOST desirable way of establishing rapport with a client who comes to the counse-   14.____
    lor with a problem is to

    A. demonstrate sincere interest in him
    B. offer to do everything possible to solve his problem for him
    C. use the language of the client
    D. promise to keep his problem confidential

15. Role playing has been used as a technique in parent education work. Of the following,   15.____
    the major value is that it

    A. permits parents to express unconscious feelings and thereby solve conflicts
    B. tells a story in a forceful and therefore lasting way
    C. provides an opportunity for the individual to view his problems by standing off and looking at them through the eyes of someone else
    D. brings to light problems people never knew they had

16. If during a counseling situation a client expressed anger about a particular situation,   16.____
    which of the following responses would a non-directive counselor MOST likely make?

    A. "Why are you so angry?"
    B. "Is there any need to get so upset about this?"
    C. "This has really made you very mad, hasn't it?"
    D. "Do you feel better now that you have expressed your anger?"

17. In a counseling process, the counselor should usually give information   17.____

    A. whenever it is needed
    B. at the end of the process
    C. in the introductory interview
    D. just before the client would ordinarily request it

18. "After having recognized and clarified feelings and conflicts, it is usually necessary to go   18.____
    beyond the stage of understanding and to elaborate a constructive plan for future action."
    Which of the following people would NOT go along with the above statement?

    A. Thorne   B. Robinson
    C. Williamson   D. Rogers

19. The counselor should focus his attention in the beginning upon   19.____

    A. the transference phenomenon
    B. evidences of hostility
    C. the unique characteristics of the particular relationship at hand
    D. indications of client aggressiveness

20. A recent guidance text that stresses the broad developments of our national heritage, our contemporary social setting, our value patterns, and also the integration into guidance of many disciplines-sociology, anthropology, philosophy, psychology-is   20._____
    A. FOUNDATIONS OF GUIDANCE - Miller
    B. GUIDANCE POLICY AND PRACTICE - Mathewson
    C. GUIDANCE IN TODAY'S SCHOOLS - Mortenson & Schmuller
    D. GUIDANCE SERVICES - Humphreys, Traxler & North

21. Which one of the following characteristics of counseling is inconsistent with the others?   21._____
    A. Counseling is more than advice-giving.
    B. Counseling involves something more than the solution to an immediate problem.
    C. Counseling concerns itself with attitudes rather than actions.
    D. Counseling involves intellectual rather than emotional attitudes as its basic raw material.

22. One approach to counseling has been labeled "non-directive". The word "non-directive" derives from the fact that, in this approach to counseling, the counselor   22._____
    A. does not tell the client what he should do
    B. makes the client responsible for the direction of the course of the interviews
    C. does not make judgments about the behavior of the client
    D. avoids possible areas of threat to the client

23. Of the following personality traits, which would be LEAST essential for an effective counselor to possess?   23._____
    A. Extroversion   B. Objectivity
    C. Security   D. Sensitivity

24. Interpretation as a therapeutic tool is considered a hindrance to therapy progress by   24._____
    A. orthodox Freudians   B. neo-analysts
    C. Rogerians   D. Adlerians

25. The current interpersonal behavior of the client is probably MOST important as a therapy topic to which two analytic theorists?   25._____
    A. Freud and Adler   B. Adler and Rank
    C. Freud and Rank   D. Horney and Sullivan

KEY (CORRECT ANSWERS)

1. B
2. D
3. D
4. B
5. C

6. B
7. A
8. B
9. B
10. C

11. A
12. B
13. D
14. A
15. C

16. C
17. A
18. D
19. C
20. A

21. D
22. B
23. A
24. C
25. D

TEST 2

DIRECTIONS: Each question or incomplete statement is followed by several suggested answers or completions. Select the one that BEST answers the question or completes the statement. *PRINT THE LETTER OF THE CORRECT ANSWER IN THE SPACE AT THE RIGHT.*

1. When a counselor is listening to a client, it is MOST important that he be able to

    A. show interest and agreement with what the client is saying
    B. paraphrase what the client is saying
    C. understand the significance of what the client is saying
    D. differentiate between fact and fiction in what the client is saying

2. On which one of the following is successful counseling LEAST likely to depend?

    A. The counselor's theoretical orientation
    B. The counselor's ability to bring the client's feelings and attitudes into the open
    C. The counselor's diagnostic ability
    D. The client's readiness for counseling

3. A client is referred to you for counseling against his will and is suspicious and uncooperative. You should

    A. explain to him that you cannot help him unless he is prepared to cooperate
    B. explain that you are not taking sides and that you will be impartial
    C. show him that you know how he feels and encourage him to talk about it
    D. explain that you are on his side and will listen sympathetically to anything that he might care to bring up

4. Which one of the following would NOT be considered a basic objective of the first interview between a client and a counselor?

    A. Beginning a sound counseling relationship
    B. Identifying the client's real problem
    C. Opening up the area of client feelings and attitudes
    D. Clarifying the nature of the counseling process for the client

5. All of the following counselor statements or actions are appropriate techniques for ending an interview EXCEPT

    A. "Our time is nearly up. Is there something else you have in mind for today?"
    B. "Let's see now. Suppose we go over what we've accomplished today."
    C. Counselor may glance at his watch and say, "When would you like to come in again?"
    D. Counselor may shuffle papers on desk and say, "Now, let's see; when is my next appointment?"

6. It has been recognized in recent literature that the value structure of the individual counselor has what kind of effect on the counseling process?

    A. Direct   B. Indirect
    C. Little   D. None

7. The intensive study of the same individuals over a fairly long period of time represents the

   A. cross-sectional approach
   B. longitudinal approach
   C. clinical approach
   D. biographical approach

8. Of the following techniques, the one which is MOST characteristic of non-directive or client-centered therapy is

   A. encouraging transference
   B. free association
   C. reflection of feeling
   D. permissive questioning

9. In making predictions about how a client will behave in a given situation, a counselor

   A. should limit himself to those situations for which "actuarial" data are available
   B. must rely on "clinical" judgment in many situations but use "actuarial" data wherever possible
   C. should rely on "clinical" judgment in all situations, since they are more valid than "actuarial" predictions
   D. always uses "actuarial" data, but modifies them in light of his "clinical" impression of the client

10. A research study that establishes an hypothesis, sets up control groups, collects data, and generalizes from the data is

    A. formulative
    B. diagnostic
    C. experimental
    D. exploratory

11. The MOST usable single index of the social and economic status of all the members of any family is

    A. occupation of the father
    B. religious affiliation of the family
    C. location of the home in the community
    D. socio-economic rating by neighbors

12. When a counselor does NOT understand the meaning of a response that a counselee has made, the counselor usually should

    A. proceed to another topic
    B. admit his lack of understanding and ask for clarification
    C. act as if he understands so that the counselee's confidence in him is not shaken
    D. ask the counselee to choose his words more carefully

13. When the counselor makes a response which touches off a high degree of resistance in the counselee, he should

    A. apologize and rephrase his remark in a less threatening manner
    B. accept the resistance
    C. ignore the counselee's resistance
    D. recognize that little more will be accomplished in the interview and offer another appointment

14. Directive and non-directive counseling are two emphases in counseling theory and practice. From the pairs of names listed below, indicate the two that are representative of the Directive school.

    A. Thorne and Williamson
    B. Rogers and Thorne
    C. Williamson and Sullivan
    D. Sullivan and Rogers

15. Rogerian counseling theory is based on the assumption that the potential and tendency for growth toward a fully functioning personality is present in

    A. a few "self-actualized" persons
    B. most people of above average intelligence
    C. people whose behavior can be considered as "normal" and socially effective
    D. all people

16. Anecdotal records should contain which type(s) of information?

    A. Evaluations
    B. Interpretations
    C. Factual reports
    D. Prognoses

17. RESISTANCE in relation to psychological counseling typically refers to the

    A. client's defenses against his inner conflicts
    B. counselor's unwillingness to deal with the client's emotional problems
    C. client's having enough ego strength so that he can face his problems
    D. counselor's having enough ego strength so that he can help the client face his problems

18. On which one of the following does the democratic leader specifically rely? His ability to

    A. listen and tactfully guide the discussion in the direction he has planned and the members' willingness to cooperate
    B. diagnose situations, to interpret and explain them to the members and their willingness to accept
    C. discern the issues which the members could profitably discuss and his willingness to allow them with his help to do so
    D. understand the meaning of the response from the member's frame of reference and his willingness for them to make decisions

19. Advisement in counseling is MOST effective when the counselee is in a state of

    A. perceiving his problem as related to a conflict with inner forces
    B. minimal conflict and of optimal readiness for action
    C. perceiving his problem as related to an external conflict
    D. feeling extremely ambivalent about his self-concept

20. Of the following, the MOST valid use of projective techniques is the study of the

    A. problems which an individual faces
    B. cultural effects upon an individual
    C. inner world of an individual
    D. human relationships of an individual

21. Diagnosis is NOT regarded as a helpful antecedent to counseling by   21.____

    A. Cottle   B. Rogers
    C. Thorne   D. Williamson

22. The beginning counselor must be alert to interferences to rapport. Which one of the following is NOT considered an intereference?   22.____

    A. Injecting the counselor's present mood
    B. Engaging in "small talk" at the start of the interview
    C. Registering surprise or dismay
    D. Emphasizing the counselor's ability

23. There is some evidence according to Rogers that counseling is more effective with   23.____

    A. younger adults or higher intelligence
    B. older adults of higher intelligence
    C. younger adults of lower intelligence
    D. older adults of lower intelligence

24. In assisting with the scheduling of interviews for educational planning, the counselor should suggest that group instruction   24.____

    A. follow the counseling interview
    B. is not necessary when individual interviews can be scheduled since each case is different
    C. precede the counseling
    D. may either precede or follow the counseling interview

25. A client has requested an interview with the counselor to discuss a personal problem. In general, the BEST way to begin the interview is to   25.____

    A. come directly to the point and encourage the client to talk about his problem
    B. assure him that everything discussed will be confidential
    C. offer to help him in every way possible
    D. inquire whether he has discussed the problem with anyone else

KEY (CORRECT ANSWERS)

1.	C	11.	A
2.	A	12.	B
3.	C	13.	B
4.	B	14.	A
5.	D	15.	D
6.	A	16.	C
7.	B	17.	A
8.	C	18.	C
9.	B	19.	B
10.	C	20.	C

21. B
22. B
23. A
24. C
25. A

EXAMINATION SECTION
TEST 1

DIRECTIONS: Each question or incomplete statement is followed by several suggested answers or completions. Select the one that BEST answers the question or completes the statement. *PRINT THE LETTER OF THE CORRECT ANSWER IN THE SPACE AT THE RIGHT.*

1. In working with adolescent groups, an important point to remember is to give

    A. guidance without taking matters out of the group's hands
    B. guidance to the youth leaders only
    C. assistance only when the groups ask for it
    D. direct assistance at every opportunity

2. The BASIC purpose to be kept in mind when programming group activities for delinquent adolescents is that

    A. group activities are natural for delinquents
    B. the activities should focus on control and discipline
    C. the youths should share in the program expenses
    D. the activities should focus on total freedom of expression

3. Workers assigned to your unit are experiencing difficulties with programming group activities. The programs seen to be out of context with the problems of the youths, and the youths are reported to be bored, evasive, and non-participating.
An important factor in programming that you, as unit supervisor, must teach them is

    A. to involve the group members in the planning and implementation of all programs
    B. to include current procedures like enounter, reality therapy, and crisis intervention
    C. that they must have individual meetings with key members to enlist their aid and assistance
    D. that they are not providing enough direction and control to the group meetings

4. The one of the following groups of characteristics which MOST correctly describes anti-social adolescent groups is

    A. fraternity, mutual respect, and interest in each other
    B. group loyalty, need to retaliate, and the necessity to fight
    C. divisiveness, mistrust, and self-centeredness
    D. none of the above

5. You are supervising a new worker who tells you, during his supervisory conference, that he feels that he has not been able to help his group to re-direct their energies into productive channels.
It would be BEST for you to advise this worker that

    A. he should not be discouraged because adolescents have boundless energy that is difficult to control
    B. adolescent groups respond to planning and direction, and that he should set up some simple form of organization
    C. the conflict and competition concept of group behavior requires group psychotherapy
    D. his anxieties are getting in the way of effective work with his group

6. A new worker in the unit under your supervision shows in his recording that he has been able to overcome his feelings of insecurity in his new role of working with his group and to work through the initial testing period imposed on him by the group. However, during his supervisory conference, you discover that he is extremely anxious because the group does not seem to be verbalizing their problems with him.
You should advise this worker in conference that

   A. these are hard-core youths who do not talk about their problems
   B. his recording is weak, and should be done in process style for the next six months
   C. his anxiety is probably being communicated to the group, inhibiting them from verbalizing their problems
   D. a marathon encounter with the group may help them to verbalize their problems

7. In preparation for a staff conference covering principles of working with alienated youth groups, you assign different aspects of the subject to different workers. In his notes, the worker who is to discuss *process in working with groups* lists the following:
   1. sensitivity to the pace of group movement
   2. resistance and resentment arising from domination by the worker
   3. time and place of meetings

   An IMPORTANT part that was omitted by the worker is

   A. realistic programming
   B. awareness of *where the group is at*
   C. the importance of sensitivity training
   D. supervision

8. A youth worker reports to you in a supervisory conference that the youths in his group are unfriendly and bossy with each other, but that when he leaves them, roughhousing breaks out.
The MOST likely explanation for this is that

   A. he is not exercising enough control
   B. he is probably too strict and tight with them
   C. this particular group of kids usually acts this way
   D. this is unusual behavior of alienated youth

9. The SIGNIFICANT factors that would distinguish a constructive and orderly group of adolescents from an anti-social gang are the

   A. aims, quality of the relationships, and behavior of the individuals
   B. aims, personality of the members, and locale
   C. age, problems, and behavior of the members
   D. locale, personality of the members, and leadership

10. Youth workers involved with groups of adolescent girls may have to deal with problems of sexual acting-out. Programming for girls involved in sexual acting-out should have as its BASIC purpose

    A. security building and developing a feeling of being needed and wanted
    B. sex information and a discussion of birth control and abortion
    C. rap sessions on dating, making out, and male-female psychology
    D. parties, dances, outings, and bus rides

11. Adolescents have many fears that they are ashamed to show because they are afraid of disapproval. Restraining these fears may lead to anxieties that could be even more troublesome.
    To help youths resolve such problems, youth service units should emphasize in their programming

    A. activities that help youths gain self-confidence
    B. rap sessions on anxiety
    C. activities that are not likely to produce fear
    D. hiking, swimming, wrestling, and basketball

11.____

12. All of the following are purposes of group counseling EXCEPT

    A. avoidance of treating pathology as such
    B. helping clients attain a better level of functioning
    C. modifying social and familial problems
    D. resolving intra-psychic conflicts

12.____

13. A MAJOR advantage of having group programs for local teenagers in Youth Services Agency neighborhood offices is that

    A. these programs are less expensive to operate
    B. the participating groups are mutual groups in their own environment
    C. this activity is necessary for suppressing riots
    D. such programs serve as good public relations

13.____

14. A worker reports about his youth council that one of the sub-groups in the council revolves around a boy who has many constructive ideas. However, this boy's participation is limited due to the rivalry between him and the elected president.
    The supervisor should advise the worker to

    A. have the leader of the sub-group excluded from the council
    B. help the leader of the sub-group participate more actively
    C. tell the leader of the sub-group to *play ball* with the rest of the council
    D. let the council settle this problem without outside assistance

14.____

15. One of your youth workers is having difficulty forming a group in a particular neighborhood. Parents in that area are upset about the idea of teenage groups. This worker plans to meet with some of these parents, and he asks your help in reaching a goal with them. As supervisor, you should advise him to approach this problem by

    A. helping the parents to see that group activities are a sign of a youth's growth, not of a lack of gratitude or affection for his parents
    B. informing the parents that it is the professional opinion of the Youth Services Agency that groups are necessary in order to serve youth constructively
    C. postponing this meeting until you can convince individual parents of the value of groups
    D. helping the parents to see that many of their teenagers are having difficulties at home and in school because they do not participate in group activities

15.____

16. Experts have described festivals, fairs, holidays, etc. as *nothing less nor more than excesses provided by law and which owe their cheerful character to the release which they bring.*
The significance of this in programming unit projects is to

    A. have the workers assist the community in sponsoring fairs, block dances, etc.
    B. leave the sponsoring of fairs, dances, etc. to associations affiliated with the police department
    C. avoid involving large groups of people in public affairs because of the danger of fights, riots, etc.
    D. use a good part of the unit's budget for fairs, dances, bazaars, etc.

17. Which one of the groups listed below has the following four characteristics:
    1. Basic depressive character
    2. Intolerance for frustration and pain
    3. Lack of meaningful objects
    4. Artificial technique to maintain self-regard?

    A. College students   B. Drug abusers
    C. Adolescents   D. Alienated youth

18. The MOST important consideration in evaluating the ego strength of an angry, deprived, mistreated, frustrated, evasive client is the client's ability to

    A. verbalize his problems
    B. redirect his anger
    C. form a relationship with an accepting worker
    D. hold a job

19. When a worker, in his first interview with a parent, tries to take down a developmental history of a boy, he usually gets many meaningless answers, such as *It was normal* or *I don't remember.*
The worker should realize that

    A. this information is inaccurate and should be disregarded
    B. the parent is under stress at first, and should be able to give more factual information later
    C. the parent purposely is withholding valuable information about the boy
    D. the parent must be told that if he cannot cooperate he cannot be helped

20. One of the workers under your supervision is puzzled as to why a mother she was working with broke off contacts prermaturely. When you read the record of this mother, you learn that she had become overdependent upon the worker before suddenly stopping her visits.
In the supervisory conference, you should help the worker to understand that this type of client

    A. is flighty, evasive, and has low reality testing
    B. is in need of deep psychotherapy
    C. is defending herself against this overdependence
    D. needs the chance to test her limits with an accepting person

21. When a worker is troubled because youths in his group ask him personal questions and he does not know how to answer them, as unit supervisor it would be BEST for you to advise the worker to

    A. interrogate the youths in detail about the reasons behind the questions
    B. tell the youths all they want to know, so that the worker appears friendly and human
    C. give a frank, brief, truthful answer and then immediately redirect the youths back to their own problems
    D. point out to the youths that the worker's personal life is not their business

22. Psychiatrists are usually concerned with the total functioning and integration of the human personality. Caseworkers usually concentrate on

    A. the same thing, but for shorter periods of time
    B. the same thing, but without prescribing medication
    C. helping the client to deal with the presenting problem
    D. all of the above

23. Some people feel that by cutting down temptations and stimuli, delinquency can be substantially decreased. Specific measures are curfews, eliminating the cruder forms of violence from the mass media, reducing the number of sexually stimulating publications available to youth, keeping down teenagers' resources for obtaining liquor, increasing recreational facilities, etc. The STRONGEST flaw in this approach is that

    A. it is not fair to non-delinquents
    B. it would not seriously affect the hard-core delinquent
    C. the community is not yet prepared for it
    D. it needs more time to prove itself

24. A COMMON error made by youth workers who are beginning to find out about the influence of unconscious desires and emotions on human behavior is to

    A. probe the client unnecessarily
    B. become over-assured that they can solve the client's problem
    C. slow up the pace of the interview
    D. look for the proper treatment method based on the client's neurosis

25. A basic technique which is used to obtain knowledge of the problem to be solved and sufficient understanding of the troubled person and of the situation, so that the problem can be solved effectively, is known as

    A. psychosomatics   B. interviewing
    C. recording   D. supervisory conferences

26. Which of the following is a CORRECT definition of the term *acceptance* as used in social work?

    A. A decision made at intake to accept the client as a case for the agency to handle
    B. The concept that the worker does not pass judgment on the client's behavior
    C. The concept of a positive and active understanding by the worker of the feelings a client expresses through his behavior
    D. Communication to the client that the worker does not condone and accept his antisocial behavior

27. Beginning youth workers are usually informed in a training session that they should be non-judgmental, should not become dependent on the client's liking them, and should not become angry. However, in an attempt to suppress these feelings, workers often behave in a stilted and artificial manner with clients.
As a supervisor, you should help your workers

   A. seek counseling to help them understand their angry feelings
   B. realize that they were not yet ready for that type of training
   C. understand that this artificiality will soon pass by as easily as it came
   D. recognize the naturalness of these feelings and learn to control their expression

28. A worker in the unit under your supervision has a youth in his group who has developed a strong antagonism toward him. You can find nothing that the worker has done to arouse such antagonism in the youth.
This antagonism is probably due to

   A. restrictions imposed on the client by the agency
   B. factors deeply hidden in the client's personality
   C. the youth's feeling of guilt because he has withheld information from the worker
   D. the fact that the worker may have promised the youth too much

29. The development of an emotional rapport, positive or negative, between the client and the worker is not abnormal, but inevitable. Sometimes the feelings that develop as a result of this rapport become excessively intense.
In those instances, the worker should

   A. request that the client be given another worker
   B. control the nature and intensity of the feelings
   C. ignore the feelings, which will disappear soon
   D. confront the client with the inappropriateness of these feelings

30. In social work, when we talk of ambivalence, we mean that the

   A. social worker refrains from imposing his moral judgments on the client
   B. supervisor assists the worker in understanding the psychological causes for client's behavior
   C. client has conflicting interests, desires, and emotions
   D. client is seeking someone who will understand the subjective reasons for his behavior

31. Although we can judge statements about objectively verifiable matters to be true or false, we are not similarly justified in passing judgments on subjective attitudes. This statement BEST explains the rationale behind the social work principle of

   A. empathy   B. self-awareness
   C. non-judgmentality   D. confidentiality

32. A psychological factor that explains why generally lawabiding individuals can become a part of a violent crowd is

   A. the deep urge for destruction and violence inherent in man
   B. the anonymity of the group would allow individuals to yield to restrained instincts
   C. that there is force in numbers, decreasing the likelihood of personal injury
   D. that man is basically a *herd animal,* so the mob is our natural environment

33. When you have learned that one of your workers has organized a protest, you should advise him to

    A. be aware that the group may not be able to defend themselves against the police
    B. alert the community to distract the police to another area
    C. call off the protest because of the probability of danger
    D. take precautions with his group in order to be sure that the protest will be orderly

34. Some local merchants are disturbed because they feel that a group of boys who *hang on the corner* will develop into a delinquent gang. They invite you, the unit supervisor, to address them at a meeting in order to describe the characteristics of delinquent gangs to them.
    In your talk to these merchants, you should

    A. describe how delinquent gangs make a career of hanging around, have a blind loyalty among members, and see destruction as their way of hitting back at society
    B. advise them to call off the meeting because the delinquent gang as such has disappeared
    C. assure them that they should not be concerned because you have a worker in that area who has this group under surveillance
    D. contact your area administrator because this involves a relationship with the community that is not on your level of responsibility

35. According to the REPORT OF THE NATIONAL ADVISORY COMMITTEE ON CIVIL DISORDERS, riots are dramatic forms of protest expressing

    A. hostility to government or private institutions
    B. undefined but real frustrations
    C. anger at the failure of society to provide certain groups with adequate opportunities
    D. all of the above

36. Many neighborhoods seem to develop a subculture in which forms of criminal and delinquent behavior and values are accepted as norms.
    If the unit area happens to be in one of these neighborhoods, the unit supervisor would be BEST advised to keep in mind that

    A. we know less about changing subcultures than we know about influencing groups and individuals
    B. it is easier to change subcultures than to influence groups and individuals
    C. subcultures are simple to identify, and helping the members to resolve their problems is comparatively easy
    D. this is only a theory and, therefore, should not influence the functioning of the unit office

37. The neighborhood drug abuse prevention network of the Addiction Services Agency is a series of broad-based community groups called

    A. CARE AND AWARE   B. EVIL AND WEAK
    C. RARE AND AWARE   D. NACE AND CARE

38. An agency whose sole purpose is to fight addiction through a comprehensive prevention and rehabilitation program is

    A. Daytop Village
    B. Narcotics Addiction Control Commission
    C. Addiction Services Agency
    D. Phoenix House

38.____

39. Agencies which have been traditionally used by the Youth Services Agency for the purpose of sponsoring approved group programs to help youth improve their behavior are:

    A. Madison-Felicia, Vocational Advisory Service, Catholic Youth Organization, United Neighborhood Houses, Federation Employment and Guidance Service, Community Centers
    B. Office of Economic Opportunity, Catholic Youth Organization, Police Athletic League, Federation Employment and Guidance Service, Vocational Advisory Service, Jewish Family Service, Federation of Protestant Welfare Agencies
    C. Catholic Youth Organization, United Neighborhood Houses, Young Men's Christian Association, Protestant Council, Police Athletic League, Builders For the Family and Youth
    D. Catholic Youth Organization, Young Men's Christian Association, Protestant Council, Police Athletic League, Office of Economic Opportunity, Builders For Family and Youth, Vocational Advisory Service

39.____

40. Agencies that are used by Youth Services Agency to provide individual casework treatment services for Youth Services Agency clients who need individual therapy for deep-seated problems are:

    A. Jewish Family Services, State Division for Youth, Catholic Charities, Staten Island Family Service, Salvation Army, Community Education
    B. Big Brothers, Catholic Charities, Jewish Board of Guardians, Jewish Family Services, Salvation Army
    C. Catholic Youth Organization, Vocational Advisory Service, Melrose Center, Federation Employment and Guidance Service, United Neighborhood Houses
    D. Catholic Charities, Jewish Family Service, Vocational Foundation, Vermont Program, Big Brothers, Boys' Harbor, Salvation Army

40.____

41. The Departments that make up the Human Resources Administration are:

    A. Manpower and Career Development, Office of Economic Opportunity, Commission on Civil Disorders, Youth Services Agency, Addiction Services, Social Services, Community Development
    B. Manpower and Career Development Agency, Office of Economic Opportunity, Youth Services Agency, Addiction Services Agency, Department of Social Services, Commission on Human Rights, Community Volunteers
    C. Human Resources Administration Central Staff, Manpower and Career Development Agency, Community Development Agency, Department of Social Services, Youth Services Agency, Addiction Services Agency, Office of Education Affairs
    D. Human Resources Administration Central Staff, Manpower and Career Development Agency, Department of Social Services, Youth Services Agency, Addiction Services Agency, Office of Economic Opportunity, Commission on Human Rights

41.____

42. A Youth Services Agency project that was developed in 1968 in response to the findings of the National Advisory Commission on Civil Disorders (Kerner-Lindsay Report) and which was designed to develop and demonstrate model approaches to engender interracial understanding between teenagers is the

    A. Youth Opportunity Center
    B. Demonstration and Training Unit
    C. Interdepartmental Neighborhood Service Center
    D. Vermont Project

42.____

43. Which one of the following is mandated to provide services to the poverty-stricken, to improve the quality of these services and the methods of delivering them, to carry out the legal commitment to the poor, and to help the poor to help themselves?

    A. Office of Economic Opportunity
    B. Environmental Resources Administration
    C. Community Action Program
    D. Model Cities Program

43.____

44. An indication of mature behavior to be sought for in the client and encouraged by the youth worker is the

    A. ability to become involved in issues of racism, urban life, and human rights
    B. development of some controls over the impulse to act out
    C. formulation of definite and specific goals in careers
    D. steady, consistent pattern of behavior that is relatively free of ambivalent feelings

44.____

45. That point in human development which marks a person's passage into adolescence is known as

    A. maturity
    B. the Oedipal stage
    C. the genital stage
    D. puberty

45.____

46. An important factor to remember about the mental, physical, social, and emotional growth of an adolescent is that the

    A. pace is uneven and individual
    B. pace is relatively even
    C. rate of growth is predictable
    D. growth has no special pattern

46.____

47. Adolescents are more likely to understand the concrete and the specific, rather than general ideas like justice, honesty, love, etc.
    The implication of this concept for the unit supervisor in guiding his staff is

    A. that programming should include recreation, job counseling, school help, and visits at times of crisis
    B. the necessity to make sure that the programs use a large part of their budget for *treats* for the youth
    C. to be sure the staff is directing much of their energy into pointing up the importance of these general concepts
    D. to help the youths understand that life has taught them to be mistrustful

47.____

48. The theory of juvenile delinquency that traces much of delinquency back to failures in family relationships during the early years of childhood, and to continuing family difficulties, offers help to the youth worker in

   A. forming a general picture of the typical delinquent
   B. understanding that fighting is one of the best ways to rise to the top
   C. identifying normal growth needs of adolescents and the obstacles against healthy maturity
   D. realizing that delinquents are children at heart and are best treated as children

49. The theory of juvenile delinquency which holds that youths from minority groups turn to anti-social behavior when they feel that their access to social, educational, and economic opportunities in legal and approved ways is blocked has had a strong impact on the establishment of agencies like the

   A. Job Corps
   B. Community Development Agency
   C. Youth Board of the 1950's
   D. Addiction Services Agency

50. Which of the following is a descriptive term for a client who is resistive, breaks appointments, withholds information, beclouds issues, relates to others in a primitive, often distorted, fashion, and acts out his wishes and conflicts in his contact with the worker?

   A. Psychotic
   B. Narcotics addict
   C. Schizophrenic
   D. Character disorder

KEY (CORRECT ANSWERS)

1. A	11. A	21. C	31. C	41. C
2. B	12. D	22. C	32. B	42. D
3. A	13. B	23. B	33. D	43. A
4. B	14. B	24. A	34. A	44. B
5. B	15. A	25. B	35. D	45. D
6. C	16. A	26. C	36. A	46. A
7. A	17. B	27. D	37. C	47. A
8. B	18. C	28. B	38. C	48. C
9. A	19. B	29. B	39. C	49. A
10. A	20. C	30. C	40. B	50. D

TEST 2

DIRECTIONS: Each question or incomplete statement is followed by several suggested answers or completions. Select the one that BEST answers the question or completes the statement. *PRINT THE LETTER OF THE CORRECT ANSWER IN THE SPACE AT THE RIGHT.*

1. Adolescents who become involved in delinquent behavior are usually angry or frustrated a large part of their time. Conscious awareness of the intensity of their needs makes them feel weak.
   For this reason, they frequently

   A. are easier to work with
   B. prefer strong male youth workers
   C. need to be controlled and disciplined
   D. have to show the world they don't care what happens

   1.____

2. Sociologists and behavioral scientists provided the ideas of cohesion, conflict, competition, cooperation, authority, leadership, and stratification that are clearly manifested in

   A. supervision B. addiction
   C. group behavior D. casework therapy

   2.____

3. The one of the following causes of juvenile delinquency among sub-lower class youth which has been given increased attention in recent years is the

   A. prevalence of the one-parent family
   B. failure of family relationships in the early years
   C. blockage of educational, vocational, and social opportunities
   D. emotional problems and psychiatric disorders of youth

   3.____

4. A high-ranking official recently stated that some youths have made suicide attempts in detention centers so that they would be transferred from the detention centers to hospitals.
   If the workers in a unit should bring this topic up for discussion in a staff meeting, the supervisor should

   A. instruct workers to inform the youths of the area about this method of getting out of a detention center
   B. have a worker visit a youth in detention in order to observe and report back to the unit so that a demonstration can be organized
   C. assign different workers to study various aspects of the problem in order to plan an intelligent, informed discussion
   D. point out that the worker does not directly become involved with this problem, and direct the discussion to a more pertinent topic

   4.____

5. The MOST significant characteristics of the daily lives of alienated youths can be described as

   A. their days are aimless, disorganized, and unproductive
   B. they spend most of their time in antisocial activity
   C. they spend a good portion of their time seeking a means of earning money
   D. they concentrate most of their energies on actingout

   5.____

6. A young man drops into the office to request help in finding a job. While he is waiting to see the office coverage worker, you notice he is nervous, sweating, yawning, and constantly blowing his nose.
   As a unit supervisor, you should

   A. overlook this because the youth is probably worried about getting a job, and is dirty and tired
   B. feel assured that the worker will observe this also and handle it in the best possible way
   C. advise the worker of your observations, and discuss the possible causes of this behavior with the worker
   D. do none of the above

7. The *battered child syndrome* is reported to be one of the most difficult problems facing health officials.
   When a worker knows of a case of a boy being severely abused physically by his parents, the supervisor should advise the worker to

   A. discuss this with a psychiatrist to find out why the parent is abusing the child
   B. tell the child to stay away from the parents as much as possible
   C. try to talk to the parents to help them see what they are doing wrong
   D. report the situation to the Bureau of Child Welfare of the Department of Social Services

8. Ghetto youth today present symptoms of delinquent behavior that are in many ways more disruptive than those of the anti-social gang members of the 1950's. Some of these symptoms are

   A. alienation, school drop-outs, drug addiction, loosely formed cliques
   B. interracial conflicts, community violence, few family ties, teenage drifters, and panhandlers
   C. promiscuity, alcoholism, vandalism, homosexuality, venereal disease
   D. all of the above

9. A psychological factor that tends to make the spread of drug abuse today easier among siblings in a family is the

   A. necessity for drug users to seduce others to join them
   B. need of siblings to rebel against parents
   C. fact that siblings can more easily *cover* for each other
   D. fact that older siblings can force younger siblings to take drugs

10. A parent complains to a worker that her teenage son is hanging around with a *bad bunch,* that money is strangely missing from the house lately, that his eating habits have changed, and that he spends long periods of time alone.
    When the worker discusses this with the unit supervisor, the supervisor should

    A. interview the parent as soon as possible to get more precise information
    B. advise the worker to refer the parent to a doctor to have her son examined
    C. help the worker to be supportive to the parent and try to make contact with the son
    D. assure him the parent is just jumpy over the drug scare and there is probably another explanation for the boy's behavior

11. A worker reports that the youths in his area think that *blowing pot* is all right because marijuana is not addictive, is harmless in small doses, and is far less dangerous than alcohol. The worker asks your help to talk the kids out of *blowing pot*.
    You, as unit supervisor, should

    A. advise the worker to refer the youths to the nearest, best drug rehabilitation resource
    B. give the worker enough literature so the youths could learn more about the situation
    C. assure the worker that these facts are true
    D. help the worker to involve the youths in constructive group activities

12. It is important for the youth worker to understand that the adolescent's FIRST loyalty belongs to his

    A. peer group
    B. siblings
    C. parents
    D. best friend

13. One of the workers in a unit office reports that he is having some difficulty with his group of youths. It is apparent that the youth leader of the group is seriously disturbed.
    The BEST action for the worker to take FIRST is to

    A. try to redirect the leader's activities into more constructive channels
    B. help the group select a leader who is more psychologically sound
    C. take steps to have the leader removed from the community into a setting where he can get psychiatric help
    D. show this leader where his behavior is hurting the group so that he can change his behavior

14. The pleasurable effect produced by heroin is the

    A. feeling of excitement and energy
    B. expansion of sense perceptions
    C. feeling of relaxation, sociability, and good humor
    D. suppression of fears, tensions, and anxieties

15. The many rumors that spread throughout the Youth Services Agency are harmful to the morale of the staff because they result in worry, suspicion, mistrust, and uncertainty. The BEST way the unit supervisor can stop a rumor is to

    A. disregard it
    B. deny it
    C. start a different one
    D. give the staff the true facts

16. Parental rejection and neglect damage the personality of the developing child, and orient the child toward his agemates in the neighborhood.
    This statement would BEST describe the mechanism that leads to

    A. delinquency in urban industrial areas
    B. the establishment of neighborhood clubs
    C. the generation gap
    D. drug addiction

17. Many young people are introduced to drugs by friends. Youths don't like to be called *chicken,* they like to be *hip* like the rest, and they have to be a part of something. When a worker asks for your guidance on handling one of his youths who is being pressured into getting *high* by his friends, as the unit supervisor, you should help the worker

   A. gradually move this youth into another group of youths who are *straight*
   B. make the worker realize this is his problem, in his area, and that he must work it out the best way
   C. involve this youth and his group of friends in the programs and activities of the unit
   D. tell the youth he must work this out himself

18. Youth workers must help angry alienated adolescents to learn how to

   A. control their anger by learning when it's worthwhile to get angry
   B. suppress their angry feelings
   C. realize that anger is an unconscious emotion
   D. take part in aggressive demonstrations and takeovers

19. Of the following, an IMPORTANT reason why certain youths are stereotyped by the police and are therefore treated unfairly by them is that

   A. delinquent youths deserve to be treated more severely because they cause trouble for others
   B. these are only allegations and rhetoric made up by revolutionary elements who are hostile to the police
   C. the prevalence of *turnstile justice* results in hasty judgments by the police
   D. police officers in the field have no immediate data concerning the youths' backgrounds and react to their behavior at the moment

20. Group approaches are COMMONLY used for

   A. encounter, discussion, training, and administration
   B. education, counseling, therapy, and recreation
   C. counseling, recreation, catharsis, and crisis intervention
   D. competition, leadership, administration, and training

21. A worker under your supervision is having difficulty reaching some of the youths he is working with on a one-to-one basis. The recording on these youths shows that they have had little opportunity for healthy interpersonal relations.
You should advise this worker to

   A. involve these youths in group counseling in order to help them overcome their reluctance in sharing experiences with another person
   B. refer these youths for psychiatric services because they are not likely to be reached by a youth worker
   C. assign these youths to Big Brothers or Big Sisters because they need to share a normal family experience
   D. give these youths more time to get to know and trust the worker

22. Planning, organization, methods, direction, coordination, budget and fiscal management, public relations, personnel administration, training, and supervision are the ESSENTIAL elements of

    A. group psychotherapy
    B. ego-oriented casework
    C. consultation
    D. administration

22._____

23. If a supervisor is unaware of a new worker's limitations and makes demands which are beyond the worker's capabilities, this will

    A. undermine the worker's confidence in functioning up to the limit of his actual capacities
    B. provide an incentive for the worker to further his training and improve services
    C. demonstrate the need for the agency to provide better orientation and in-service training for staff
    D. encourage the worker to function at a level higher than his present capacities

23._____

24. A high government official has announced: *We're looking for possible consolidation of services, for overlapping, for frills, for some built-in bureaucratic procedures that have been kind of historic but that no one has ever taken a long look at to see if time and technology have made them obsolete.*
    For the unit supervisor, the implication of this statement is that it is his responsibility to

    A. ignore this announcement since it pertains to matters beyond his responsibility
    B. report all matters of bureaucratic inefficiency directly to this high government official
    C. inform his workers at a staff meeting that there will be no funds for programs for the next few months
    D. try to involve the staff in a realistic reappraisal of the unit's program and discuss suggestions for cutbacks with the area administrator

24._____

25. Assume that you are a new unit supervisor in the Youth Services Agency and your workers bring many grievances to your attention.
    The BEST way for you, the supervisor, to reduce grievances in your unit is to

    A. have the workers submit fully documented written grievances
    B. consider each grievance seriously and eliminate the cause if possible
    C. make workers realize that grievances reflect their immaturity and rejection of authority
    D. refer the workers' grievances to the area Administrator

25._____

26. Of the following, BASIC subject areas to be discussed in staff conferences are:

    A. Job responsibilities, agency structure, social work concepts, needs and resources of people
    B. Case-studying, interviewing, individual growth and development, sources of information other than the client
    C. Community resources, work organization, child welfare services, and standards of performance
    D. All of the above

26._____

27. The discussion method in teaching provides a way to help staff integrate knowledge and thus make it available for application to day-to-day work.
To help workers integrate knowledge and develop skill is an IMPORTANT aspect of

   A. professional training
   B. memos, directives, and position papers
   C. staff and individual conferences
   D. job descriptions

28. The subjects of discussion in staff meetings cannot be isolated from what the unit supervisor

   A. thinks is most important
   B. reads in books, journals, etc.
   C. hears at supervisors' meetings
   D. discusses in individual conferences

29. Interplay between persons appears to speed up the learning process; discussion of the material provides an opportunity for a sharing of knowledge and experience and allows for a testing out of new ideas and application of theory.
These are the objectives for

   A. Sensitivity Training
   B. T-Groups
   C. Staff Conferences
   D. Administrative Training

30. A leadership which aims to develop the individual staff member's skill and knowledge, and to direct activities of the staff in such a way as to bring about improvements in the agency's services given to the client. This is a description of GOOD

   A. staff development
   B. psychological direction
   C. public accountability
   D. supervision

31. In addition to familiarity with techniques in administrative planning and professional knowledge, the MOST important element in good supervision in a social agency is skill in

   A. office management
   B. human relations
   C. business methods
   D. psychological evaluation

32. If an agency does not have clear and specific unit and job functions, the MOST probable result will be

   A. a gross breakdown in services
   B. gaps and overlaps in responsibility and authority
   C. an inability to function according to the city charter
   D. a violation of the union contractual agreement

33. The one of the following which is the MOST important thing for a unit supervisor to keep in mind regarding the organizational structure of his unit is the

   A. preparation of time sheets and monthly reports
   B. two-way communication and maximum delegation
   C. geometric executive relationships
   D. critiques and controls

34. Budget and fiscal management is one essential practice of administration. A unit supervisor should see budgeting and fiscal management as a

    A. planning instrument
    B. fiscal control
    C. mandate from the civil service commission
    D. prerequisite of a union contractual agreement

34._____

35. Public relations with the community is one of the responsibilities of the unit supervisor. Good public relations means

    A. organizing the community to put pressure on officials in behalf of the agency
    B. getting reports from workers about the malcontents in the community and dealing with them in a diplomatic manner
    C. assuring the community that the unit will provide staff to problem areas
    D. getting understanding and cooperation from the community with which the agency is concerned

35._____

36. Problems and misunderstandings that arise from the lack of effective intraorganizational communication are apparent in many organizations.
    Of the following, the means to be employed by the unit supervisor to establish effective communication are

    A. supervisory and staff conferences
    B. manuals, bulletins, and periodic reports
    C. bulletin boards, memos, and unit newsletters
    D. all of the above

36._____

37. A personnel problem facing supervisors in public service more than in private industry is

    A. union management and negotiation
    B. budget and fiscal control
    C. systematic selection and tenure
    D. advisory boards and political connections

37._____

38. Which of the following three types of records are COMMON to most social agencies?

    A. Administrative, budgetary, and case
    B. Administrative, statistical, and case
    C. Administrative, budgetary, and statistical
    D. Budgetary, statistical, and case

38._____

39. Even after several supervisory conferences on a case, a worker in your unit seems not to be giving effective help. In a burst of anger, the worker tells a coworker that the supervisor expects him to learn in a short time what the supervisor has taken years to learn.
    Of the following, the BEST description of the supervisory relationship here is that the

    A. supervisor is so intent on seeing that the necessary service is given that he is unaware of the worker's inability to perform the service
    B. worker's behavior shows that he is too immature to be working in such a difficult field

39._____

C. worker is unaware of casework principles and techniques and their application to such a difficult case
D. supervisor is unable to give the worker effective guidance in the supervisory conference, which indicates that the worker needs academic professional training

40. The one of the following which is NOT an essential ingredient of a good staff development and training program is that it should

   A. include all members of the agency
   B. meet the specific needs of the staff in relation to their job responsibilities
   C. be a continuing process
   D. give out the necessary rules and regulations of the agency

41. One of the areas in which consultation differs from supervision is that consultation

   A. is not in the direct administrative line of authority
   B. is offered by someone skilled in a specific area
   C. relates to procedure rather than function
   D. requires special training

42. The supervisor should make sure the unit office keeps records about the youths it serves and their families since these records help in diagnosing and understanding the problems.
Of the following, as the PRIMARY source of information for case records, the workers should use

   A. reports from psychiatrists, doctors, etc.
   B. all other agencies involved with the family
   C. teachers, friends, local indigenous leaders
   D. the parents and the youths themselves

43. Statistical records are needed for planning, research, and accountability although many workers feel that statistics are dull and boring. On the unit level, statistics can come alive when they are

   A. recorded in non-technical language
   B. compiled by the unit expert in mathematics
   C. collected selectively and used against a background knowledge of the community
   D. elaborate, detailed, and accurate

44. With the passage of time, case records

   A. become more valuable
   B. decline in usefulness
   C. produce more information
   D. become cumulative records

45. In general, the purpose of a case record is to

   A. improve staff training and development
   B. make statistics pertinent and real
   C. provide data for research
   D. further professional service to a client

46. A unit supervisor finds after an intensive in-service training course in case recording that his workers tend to postpone their recording and summaries.
    The MOST likely explanation for this is that

    A. recording is not valuable enough to waste that amount of time on
    B. sufficient leadership was not given in the development of case records
    C. the workers are too busy in the field to have time to record
    D. the latest trend in social work is towards shorter records

47. A unit supervisor who has fewer youth workers in his unit than he can supervise effectively will be likely to

    A. make his staff overdependent on him
    B. lack the desire to train his workers effectively
    C. confuse his staff because of lack of direction
    D. supervise his staff too closely

48. The one of the following which is MOST likely to be seriously impaired as a result of poor supervision is the

    A. attitude of youth workers
    B. area of inter-departmental relations
    C. maintenance of case records and reports
    D. staff training and development program

49. It is generally good practice for the supervisor to ask for the opinions of his staff members before taking action affecting them.
    The GREATEST disadvantage of following this principle when changing schedules or assignments is that staff may

    A. believe that the supervisor is unable to make his own decisions
    B. take advantage of the opportunity to present grievances during the discussion
    C. be resentful if their suggestions are not accepted
    D. suggest the same action as the supervisor had planned to take

50. The expansion of community relations or human relations units is a development resulting from the ghetto riots of the past few years.
    The MOST important function such a unit can perform is to

    A. preach brotherhood and racial equality
    B. serve as a means for local city agency officials to develop city policy in accordance with local needs
    C. serve as a means of communication between people with grievances and policy makers who can take action
    D. give awards to prominent citizens who have promoted inter-racial understanding

KEY (CORRECT ANSWERS)

1. D	11. D	21. A	31. B	41. A
2. C	12. A	22. D	32. B	42. D
3. C	13. C	23. A	33. B	43. C
4. C	14. D	24. D	34. A	44. B
5. A	15. D	25. B	35. D	45. D
6. C	16. A	26. D	36. D	46. B
7. D	17. C	27. C	37. C	47. D
8. D	18. A	28. D	38. B	48. A
9. A	19. D	29. C	39. A	49. C
10. C	20. B	30. D	40. A	50. C

EXAMINATION SECTION
TEST 1

DIRECTIONS: Each question or incomplete statement is followed by several suggested answers or completions. Select the one that BEST answers the question or completes the statement. *PRINT THE LETTER OF THE CORRECT ANSWER IN THE SPACE AT THE RIGHT.*

1. The peer group serves the individual in the socialization process by 1._____

    A. showing him how to relate to other groups
    B. showing him how to be mature
    C. helping him to achieve an identity for himself
    D. helping him accept the discipline of his family

2. The age at which intelligence tests yield the MOST reliable prediction of future academic performance is 2._____

    A. 2-4 B. 4-6 C. 6-8 D. 12-14

3. Many studies have explored the effects of maternal deprivation on children. The findings indicate that such deprived children are MOST likely to be 3._____

    A. independent and active
    B. inert, withdrawn, mentally retarded and physically inferior
    C. less prone to infectious diseases because there is less danger of infection from others
    D. socially responsive to other adults

4. Of the following, which is MOST characteristic of the late maturing adolescent boy? 4._____

    A. Better adjustment to his age mates
    B. Greater independence of others
    C. Better acceptance of discipline
    D. Consistently negative evaluation of himself

5. Of the following, the major cause of juvenile delinquency is 5._____

    A. parental rejection   B. poverty
    C. culture conflict   D. inferior biological structure

6. In the recent research and study concerning the learning of disadvantaged youth, the MOST important single finding has been that 6._____

    A. the pre-school is the level of education which must be expanded
    B. the mother is the key factor in the enrichment of the socially disadvantaged
    C. the model the child identifies with must be well chosen
    D. little can be done for delinquent girls after seventeen years of age

7. An author who concerns himself with the "epigenetic principle of gradual unfoldings," the principle that the successive differentiations made during a lifetime provide a person with a developmental concept of self, is 7._____

    A. Esther Lloyd-Jones   B. Erik Erikson
    C. John Dewey   D. Edmund G. Williamson

63

8. The belief that power and status motives are MORE significant for behavior than broadly sexual motives was advocated by

   A. Freud
   B. Adler
   C. Jung
   D. Rank

9. Of all children, what percentage is generally considered to be mentally retarded?

   A. .5 B. 3.0 C. 10.0 D. 15.0

10. Studies of social acceptance show that gifted children are

    A. less socially acceptable than the average
    B. more socially acceptable than the retarded but less socially acceptable than the average
    C. more socially acceptable than the average and far more than the retarded
    D. no more socially accepted than the average

11. Of the following, the major characteristic of autistic type schizophrenic children is

    A. psychosomatic symptoms
    B. extreme withdrawal tendencies
    C. psychopathic symptoms
    D. extreme suspiciousness of adults

12. Of the following, the protective test MOST useful in studying the body-image of crippled children is the

    A. CHILDREN'S APPERCEPTION TEST
    B. BLACKY TEST
    C. MACHOVER DRAW-A-PERSON
    D. HOUSE-TREE-PERSON

13. The MOST serious problem for the cerebral palsied which contributes to learning difficulty in school, next to speech, is

    A. defective vision
    B. left-handedness
    C. hearing
    D. hand and eye coordination

14. Of the following symptoms, which is MOST characteristic of brain damaged children?

    A. Perseveration
    B. Echolalia
    C. Hallucinations
    D. Anorexia

15. Of the following, the organization that would be MOST helpful in working with a child suffering from athetosis would be the

    A. Association for the Help of Retarded Children
    B. United Cerebral Palsy Association
    C. Parents' Association for CRMD
    D. League for Epilepsy

16. The behavior patterns that develop during adolescence are

    A. genetically determined
    B. culturally determined
    C. physiologically determined
    D. found in all societies

17. According to Erikson, if a child has his needs thoroughly satisfied during his childhood, he is *most likely* to be an adolescent who is

    A. over-demanding
    B. unable to meet frustration
    C. over-achieving
    D. successful in personal-social development

18. Research evidence on girls' fears indicates that their fears during the oepidal period involve the type of anxiety known as

    A. separation
    B. fixation
    C. castration
    D. deprivation

19. In the University of Chicago study on identical twins reared apart, the GREATEST similarity found was in

    A. intelligence
    B. vocational choice
    C. personality
    D. physical appearance

20. In which of the following groups of adolescents are personal problems in adjustment MOST likely to arise?

    A. Early maturing boys and girls
    B. Late maturing boys and girls
    C. Early maturing girls and late maturing boys
    D. Late maturing girls and early maturing boys

21. The adolescent gang structure fulfills the unsatisfied needs of lower class youth through his acquisition of

    A. social skills
    B. intellectual and vocational interests
    C. athletic skills
    D. sanctions for his own aggression

22. The major limitation of the sociogram and sociometric test is that it does NOT disclose the

    A. status of the individual
    B. variety of choice
    C. organization pattern
    D. factors underlying choice

23. In establishing identity and sex role, the adolescent is MOST likely to be influenced by which of the following?

    A. Parents
    B. Siblings
    C. Peers
    D. Teachers

24. Studies on the characteristics of intellectually dull adolescents indicate

    A. inferior physical development on the part of the dull as compared with normal children
    B. more frequent eye, ear and speech defects among the dull children
    C. no clear social or emotional difference between dull and normal children
    D. all of the above characteristics to be true

25. "I made the varsity basketball and football teams but the coach cut me off the track squad." This statement embodies which of the following ego-defense mechanisms?

    A. Projection
    B. Sublimation
    C. Repression
    D. Regression

26. Considering the various informal groups which exist in a school system, such as faculty friendship groups, student clubs, cliques, and gangs, it is noticeable that the members of each group tend to possess common information and common ideas in many respects. These group beliefs exist because

    A. of the initial self-selection of the group by its members
    B. information is filtered through group leaders
    C. members are subjected to the same range of information
    D. all of the above are true

27. Of the following, the information that a sociogram does NOT reveal is the

    A. general pattern of group organization
    B. network of group communication
    C. reasons for choices and rejections
    D. relative strength of choice status of individual members

28. The weaknesses in cross-sectional studies of adolescents lie in the fact that

    A. only those who survive through the high school are sampled
    B. only the lower levels of the socio-economic groups are sampled
    C. only some interrelationships of the aspects of growth are studied
    D. the lower levels of ability are also sampled

29. The stimulus-response theory of learning explains behavior in terms of

    A. subliminal motivational cues
    B. heredity and environment
    C. physiological processes
    D. learning by insight

30. Of the following, the major weakness of a sociometric test of social acceptability that asks only for positive choices is that it

    A. has a bad mental hygiene effect on the class
    B. crystallizes the groups' opinions of each other
    C. will give a good picture of the children in the middle range of acceptability
    D. fails to distinguish between the "overlooked" children and those who are rejected

31. In "Jonesville," middle class adolescents asked to name their best friends usually chose someone

    A. of their own social class
    B. of higher status than their own
    C. below them in social status
    D. they liked for personal reasons; their choices were distributed among all social classes

31.____

32. A common change in the personality defenses of the adolescent child is the development of

    A. greater intellectualism and isolation of affect
    B. a tendency toward avoidance and denial
    C. suspicion and withdrawal
    D. repression and literal-mindedness

32.____

33. Studies on the development of sex characteristics during pubescent growth indicate that

    A. the sequence in the development of sex characteristics is marked by great consistency
    B. the age at which specific sex characteristics appear is quite reliable
    C. the only differences in the age occurrence of specific characteristics is due to sex differences
    D. there is little range in size or variability of sex characteristics

33.____

34. Adler, Horney, and Rank are deviationists from which one of the following theories?

    A. Psychoanalytical   B. Rogerian
    C. Communications   D. Neobehavioral

34.____

35. All of the following are identified with behavioral counseling EXCEPT

    A. Williamson   B. Skinner
    C. Eysenck   D. Krumboltz

35.____

36. All of the following associations are correct EXCEPT

    A. endomorphy - softness and spherical appearance
    B. mesomorphy - hard and rectangular physique with a predominance of bone and muscle
    C. ectomorphy - a linear and fragile physique
    D. gynandromorphy - a physique that represents an exaggeration of sexual characteristics associated with the given sex

36.____

37. Psychiatrists generally agree that the three characteristics *usually* combined in a severely troubled child are

    A. laziness, hostility, withdrawal
    B. slight height, overweight, pallor
    C. lack of relatedness, a speech problem, an eating problem
    D. undernourishment, fatigue, lack of coordination

37.____

38. Directing an emotion toward a safe or acceptable object as a substitute for a dangerous or unacceptable object is a fairly good definition for which one of the following defense mechanisms?

    A. Displacement
    B. Repression
    C. Identification
    D. Rationalization

39. The "latency period" as a concept of psychoanalysis has reference to the

    A. years between early childhood and adolescence
    B. period during which successful toilet training (accommodation to time, place and manner) is normally achieved
    C. period during which the oedipal strivings reach their peak
    D. period of pubertal development

40. An unpopular girl frequently calls attention to the social deficiencies in others. Her behavior illustrates

    A. regression
    B. projection
    C. repression
    D. rationalization

41. Which one of the following was NOT supported by Kurt Lewin's research?

    A. People are more apt to change if they participate in a decision to change.
    B. It is easier to change individuals in a group situation rather than singly.
    C. Change brought about through groups was more lasting than that brought about singly.
    D. While pressures of group members upon individuals were very strong, they were not as influential as those of group leaders.

42. A six-year-old child should normally be expected to do all of the following EXCEPT

    A. play simple games
    B. put on a sweater without help
    C. draw with a crayon
    D. write in sentences

43. An educational television program developed especially for pre-school age children is

    A. Learning Your A B C's
    B. Sesame Street
    C. The Number Game
    D. The Partridge Family

44. Which of the following statements concerning masturbation in children is NOT true?

    A. Excessive masturbation can injure a child's genitals.
    B. Masturbation is practiced by most children at some point of their development.
    C. Masturbation may be a symptom of tenseness and nervousness in a child.
    D. There tends to be an increased urge to masturbate during adolescence.

45. A child's rate of physical growth is MOST rapid during the period

    A. from birth to two years
    B. from six to nine years
    C. of pre-adolescence
    D. of adolescence

46. In planning activities for a group of ten-year-old children, the children's counselor should

   A. encourage the children to participate in the planning
   B. schedule activities that are the easiest to plan
   C. realize that children at this age like to watch television
   D. insist that each child participate in each activity

47. A child of twelve would be MOST likely to find an outlet for his aggressive tendencies in

   A. watching television
   B. participating in athletics
   C. reading a history book
   D. playing checkers

48. Of the following, the statement which MOST accurately describes the physical development of boys and girls during adolescence is that

   A. girls generally mature earlier than boys
   B. boys generally mature earlier than girls
   C. boys and girls generally mature at about the same age
   D. physically active boys and girls generally mature earlier than physically inactive ones

49. The average child has not developed all the many abilities needed for beginning reading until the age of about

   A. two   B. four   C. six   D. eight

50. Which of the following situations indicates that the child is probably emotionally disturbed?

   A. A five-year-old girl suddenly starts behaving like a baby after the birth of her sister.
   B. A four-year-old boy keeps asking for his father, although he has been told repeatedly that his father has died.
   C. A ten-year-old boy has refused to play with other children since he first entered school five years ago.
   D. All of the above

KEY (CORRECT ANSWERS)

1. C	11. B	21. D	31. B	41. D
2. C	12. C	22. D	32. A	42. D
3. B	13. D	23. C	33. A	43. B
4. D	14. A	24. D	34. A	44. A
5. A	15. B	25. A	35. A	45. A
6. A	16. B	26. D	36. D	46. A
7. B	17. D	27. C	37. C	47. B
8. B	18. C	28. A	38. A	48. A
9. B	19. D	29. C	39. A	49. C
10. C	20. C	30. D	40. B	50. C

TEST 2

DIRECTIONS: Each question or incomplete statement is followed by several suggested answers or completions. Select the one that BEST answers the question or completes the statement. *PRINT THE LETTER OF THE CORRECT ANSWER IN THE SPACE AT THE RIGHT.*

1. The process by which children take to themselves the values, the thinking, and social behavior of their parents is called

    A. projection
    B. identification
    C. fixation
    D. sublimation

2. Of the following, the characteristic that MOST clearly differentiates primary drives from secondary drives is that primary drives

    A. are related to biological needs that must be satisfied
    B. are learned early in the developmental cycle
    C. are derived from complex patterns of behavior
    D. may be observed after biological needs have been met

3. Spitz and Goldfarb, in two different studies, have suggested that children who will have predictably lower I.Q's are those reared in

    A. institutions
    B. broken homes
    C. foster homes
    D. middle class homes

4. One of the MOST common fears of early childhood is the fear of

    A. animals
    B. being separated from parents
    C. being rejected by peers
    D. having too much independence

5. The average child shows the FIRST signs of laughing responses

    A. before the age of six months
    B. between the ages of six months and one year
    C. at the age of about one year
    D. at the age of about fifteen months

6. A child is LEAST likely to choose a child of the opposite sex to play with at the age of

    A. two
    B. four
    C. seven
    D. ten

7. When toilet training a two-year-old child, the children's counselor should

    A. scold the child when she wets her pants
    B. take the child to the bathroom only when she asks to go
    C. have the child sit on the toilet for long periods of time
    D. keep the toilet training routine free from tension

8. The average child of three years MOST often shows his anger by

   A. breaking things
   B. crying
   C. threatening his mother
   D. sulking

9. Children at the age of two or three occasionally have temper tantrums when they do not get what they want. Of the following, the BEST method for a children's counselor to use when faced with a temper tantrum by a two-year-old child in her group is to

   A. allow the child to have what he wants
   B. try to reason with the child by explaining why he cannot have what he wants
   C. wait until the worst of the temper tantrum is over and then make a friendly gesture toward the child
   D. order the child to stop this behavior

10. All of the following are good principles to follow in administering punishment to a three-year-old child EXCEPT the

    A. punishment should be administered immediately after the incident of bad behavior
    B. child should be punished only if he understands why his behavior was bad
    C. specific punishment should be appropriate to the specific case of bad behavior
    D. punishment should be administered in an impartial manner

11. Helen, a 14-year-old girl, has two younger sisters who are more successful than she in school. Her mother complains that at home Helen constantly makes remarks intended to hurt their feelings. Helen's behavior is BEST characterized as a form of

    A. compulsion   B. sublimation
    C. rationalization   D. projection

12. Overlearning is primarily an outgrowth of

    A. removal of inhibitions   B. additional practice
    C. strong motivation   D. fear of failure

13. "The mind responds to relationships, not to fixed stimuli" is associated with the movement in psychology known as

    A. associationism   B. behaviorism
    C. Gestalt psychology   D. functionalism

14. Which one of the following is an example of "projection"?

    A. Calling other people hostile although the hostility is within oneself
    B. Playing sick in order to avoid responsibility
    C. Kicking the desk when one really wants to kick the teacher
    D. Giving other than the true reason for one's behavior

15. The basketball player who was dropped from the squad says, "Now I'll have time to study." If he really wanted to make the team, he is

    A. regressing   B. repressing
    C. projecting   D. rationalizing

16. Which one of the following reactions is generally instigated by frustration?

    A. Tolerance
    B. Aggression
    C. Identification
    D. Avoidance

17. A patient asserts, "I can't stand the agony I suffer when I go against my mother's wishes." The therapist replies, "You really like to punish that momma inside of you for your dependency, don't you?" This response can be viewed as an example of

    A. reassurance
    B. interpretation
    C. support
    D. reflection of feeling

18. A shy young first-grade boy becomes extremely attached to his teacher. He brings her presents, asks her to help him with his clothing a great deal, and wants to sit near her all the time. He is MOST likely manifesting the mental mechanism of

    A. introjection
    B. sublimation
    C. reaction-formation
    D. transference

19. When Billy was told he could not have a cookie, he lay down on the floor and pounded it with his fists. This could be an example of

    A. repression
    B. inhibition
    C. overcompensation
    D. regression

20. Habit formations in children such biting nails, picking at sores, masturbating, etc. are generally the result of

    A. poor parental supervision and training
    B. local irritations
    C. impaired general health
    D. emotional tensions

21. The attention span of a young child

    A. is not related to his mental ability
    B. can be increased if he has a high I.Q.
    C. cannot be changed before the child learns to read
    D. can be increased if the child is interested in what he is doing

22. Most young children need

    A. few media of expression
    B. to engage in independent planning
    C. many concrete experiences
    D. generalized explanations

23. The person with whom it is MOST important for a five-year-old child to have a good adjustment is

    A. father
    B. mother
    C. teacher
    D. sibling

24. At five, the normal, average child is able to play BEST

    A. alone
    B. in a large group
    C. with one other child somewhat older than himself
    D. in a small group of five or six children

25. Good education for five-year-old children stresses the importance of

    A. learning to sit still and wait for a turn
    B. opportunities to develop skill in crafts
    C. opportunities to explore and experiment
    D. learning to walk with a partner in line

26. Motor activities figure MOST importantly in a young child's intellectual enterprises because, through them, he

    A. learns how to meet new situations successfully
    B. acquires concepts of size, shape, balance, proportion
    C. learns how to live happily with other children
    D. gains confidence in himself as a person

27. Children can BEST be helped to make good choices through

    A. play with peers
    B. many experiences in making choices
    C. absorbing the teacher's sense of values
    D. imitating other children older than they

28. The timid, shy child who hesitates to join in activities and use of materials

    A. should be left alone
    B. should be praised for the work he does by himself
    C. should be drawn into the group and encouraged to participate as often as possible
    D. should have his mother come to his class to visit so that he will have a feeling of security

29. To understand the emotional life of the adolescent, it is MOST important to

    A. appraise the adolescent's emotions in the light of our own experience
    B. take into account the many forces, apparent as well as hidden, that operate in his life
    C. overlook impulsive behavior without apparent motive
    D. draw up a scholastic profile

30. The youngster who says, "I got an A in mathematics, but the teacher gave me a D in reading," is manifesting behavior which may be termed

    A. identification   B. projection
    C. regression   D. repression

31. Of the following comments which might be made by a teacher to a boy who has just misbehaved, the one likely to be MOST effective in correcting the behavior is:

    A. You are a bad boy who likes to misbehave.
    B. You are a silly boy and don't know how to behave.
    C. You are a poor, foolish boy who will get in trouble.
    D. You are a good boy but you made a mistake.

32. The personality development of young children is hampered MOST by

    A. the lack of good schools manned by adequately educated teachers
    B. dissension in the family
    C. the lack of love and affection
    D. failure in school

33. It has been found that the gap between ability and achievement is generally SMALLEST in the

    A. gifted pupil
    B. dull pupil
    C. average pupil
    D. pupil of high socio-economic background

34. Extreme deviations in motor, adaptive, or language expression or personal-social behavior are

    A. a definite indication that a child is subnormal
    B. cause for alarm on the part of parent and teacher
    C. an indication of a temporary maladjustment
    D. reasons for seeking the advice of a specialist

35. Children's groups about the age of two typically show

    A. much cooperation
    B. sex segregation
    C. parallel activity
    D. all of these

36. Play and reading interests of boys and girls will be found to be MOST different at the age of

    A. three years
    B. six years
    C. ten years
    D. twelve years

37. As children in groups with very limited environments, such as canal-boat dwellers, "hollow-folk," etc., grow older, their I.Q. is found to

    A. increase
    B. increase greatly
    C. stay the same
    D. decrease

38. Transfer from one subject to another or to life situations will be increased if

    A. techniques and applications are emphasized
    B. the first subject is very difficult
    C. a good deal of drill is given in the first subject
    D. the situations seem quite different

39. A contemporary book by Sheldon and Eleanor Glueck reports their findings of a careful research study of juvenile delinquents. They state that

    A. most of their delinquents showed anti-social behavior beginning with their sixth year
    B. most of their delinquents did not show anti-social behavior until after their eleventh year
    C. the delinquents showed more physical defects than non-delinquents
    D. prediction tables can help to detect potential delinquents

40. Finger sucking in early childhood has long been a subject of discussion among psychiatrists. The one of the following statements which is GENERALLY accepted as true is that
    A. finger sucking denotes pending neuroses and the parents need psychiatric consultation
    B. finger sucking is a normal activity of early childhood and should not be interfered with
    C. finger sucking alters the child's facial contours and should be heavily discouraged
    D. finger sucking by a child over nine months old is due to emotional upset and needs treatment

KEY (CORRECT ANSWERS)

1.	B	11.	D	21.	D	31.	D
2.	A	12.	B	22.	C	32.	C
3.	A	13.	C	23.	B	33.	B
4.	B	14.	A	24.	D	34.	D
5.	A	15.	D	25.	C	35.	C
6.	D	16.	B	26.	B	36.	D
7.	D	17.	B	27.	B	37.	D
8.	B	18.	D	28.	C	38.	A
9.	C	19.	D	29.	B	39.	D
10.	B	20.	D	30.	B	40.	B

EXAMINATION SECTION
TEST 1

DIRECTIONS: Each question or incomplete statement is followed by several suggested answers or completions. Select the one that BEST answers the question or completes the statement. *PRINT THE LETTER OF THE CORRECT ANSWER IN THE SPACE AT THE RIGHT.*

1. The individual who emerges as the leader of a group is *usually*

    A. the person who, in the judgment of the group, can best meet the demands of the particular problem
    B. superior to the other members of the group in a wide variety of abilities
    C. chosen on the basis of personal qualities rather than ability
    D. the same person, no matter in what activities the group participates

2. The status of an individual in a group is determined, *for the most part,* by

    A. the possession of those qualities the group deems important
    B. his socio-economic level
    C. his status in other groups of which he is a member
    D. the amount of time and energy he is willing to devote to the purposes of the group

3. Among the following, the LEAST valid goal for the group discussion leader during the *first* sessions with the group is

    A. realization by the group of the distinction between an individual and his unacceptable behavior
    B. encouragement of self-revelation
    C. freedom to express any ideas or feelings for consideration by the group
    D. establishment of goals of mutual helpfulness

4. Among the following, the LEAST valid way for the counselor to encourage a sense of acceptance on the part of everyone in the group is to

    A. be nonjudgmental with respect to all contributions from the group
    B. use the technique of reflection to help clarify statements
    C. give advice when the need is apparent
    D. call attention to existing limits when necessary

5. The MOST distinctive characteristic of group counseling with younger children is the

    A. use of objects and play
    B. setting of the group
    C. lack of verbal communication
    D. non-directive role of the counselor

6. Recent studies of individuals working in groups and individuals working alone have shown that

    A. elementary school clients work better alone; junior high school clients work better in groups
    B. the quality of work completed by a given individual is much the same whether he works alone or as a member of a group

C. larger groups do better work than smaller groups working on similar tasks
D. individuals working in groups will show a high level of performance only when a group goal serves as a motivating force

7. New standards are MOST readily accepted by the members of groups when those members

   A. share in developing and establishing the standards
   B. personally know the leader who advocates the standards
   C. belong to an in-group which advocates the standards
   D. appreciate the weaknesses of the older standards

8. Group counseling differs from group therapy in that transference

   A. is interpreted in group counseling and not in group therapy
   B. is non-existent in group counseling
   C. is understood in group counseling but not interpreted
   D. reactions are discouraged in group therapy

9. Which one of the following objectives BEST describes the goal of group counseling?

   A. Broadening occupational horizons
   B. Use of peer group pressure
   C. Attitude change
   D. Helping larger numbers of people

10. In group counseling, the MOST effective communication results when the counselor-leader

    A. attempts to maintain one-way communication with individual group members
    B. becomes a member of the group and encourages two-way communication among all the members of the group including himself
    C. maintains two-way communication with individual clients and also permits some communication among clients on a rather formal basis
    D. tries to develop two-way communication with individual clients

11. "Group Dynamics" means a variety of things to many people. Which of the following is the soundest concept of the term?

    A. The structure of the group
    B. The techniques used in the group situation
    C. The factors making for productivity or failure
    D. The forces operating in the group situation

12. A group project should be defined as "multiple counseling" only if

    A. more than two group members achieve therapeutic relationships with the counselor
    B. there is a leader-participant relationship in group meetings
    C. it improves skills in human relationships
    D. individual counseling accompanies the group activity

13. Group counseling as a technique is MOST similar to which one of the following? 13.____

    A. Group guidance B. Socio-drama
    C. Social group work D. Group therapy

14. Of the following, what kind of behavior is usually manifested by the group working with a counselor in the first stages of small group sessions? 14.____

    A. Blocking B. Externalizing
    C. Rejecting D. Accepting

15. Role playing can be used effectively in group dynamics when 15.____

    A. real acting ability is present
    B. the player identifies spontaneously in feeling or attitude with real or imagined persons
    C. situations to be dramatized are carefully planned, structured and resolved
    D. there are no conflicts in behavior or differences of opinion

16. In grouping maladjusted individuals for group counseling, the MOST important criterion, of the following, is homogeneity of 16.____

    A. intelligence B. social maturity
    C. personality deviations D. age

17. Of the following, the area of guidance which lends itself LEAST readily to group study and discussion is 17.____

    A. educational and vocational opportunities
    B. problems involving family relationships
    C. questions dealing with male-female relations
    D. problems involving deep-seated emotional disturbance

18. Which one of the following "suggestions to group leaders" should be AVOIDED? 18.____

    A. Prepare a "hidden agenda" for the group session and make sure it is executed.
    B. Allow minority views to be expressed.
    C. Help all group members to grow through contributing their best services to the group.
    D. Encourage individual group members to experiment with enacting the leader role.

19. Although therapists differ in their ideas about the ideal composition for a therapeutic group, which one of the following characteristics would they agree they prefer to EXCLUDE from their groups? 19.____

    A. Silent people B. Compliant individuals
    C. Chronic monopolists D. Noisy people

20. Upon entering a classroom during group guidance period, you find the clients spontaneously acting out a home situation involving a quarrel over going to the movies. You may MOST reasonably conclude that they are 20.____

    A. using the socio-drama to work out an understanding of their home relationships
    B. spending the time in free activity for the development of social attitudes
    C. performing a psychodrama for the solution of their personal problems
    D. preparing a play to be performed in the institution's auditorium

21. Which of the following groups of descriptions BEST describes group counseling?   21.____

    A. 1. A group goal is established.
       2. Ideas associated with the goal are linked together
       3. Thought related to the goal is stimulated.
    B. 1. Listening is directed toward the understanding of ideas.
       2. The expression of problem-solving ideas is encouraged.
       3. A summary is provided as required.
    C. 1. Relevant information is supplied.
       2. The endeavour is made to reach a consensus.
       3. Ideas are reflected and clarified as necessary.
    D. 1. Listen to understand the meaning to each individual of his expression.
       2. Endeavour to further feeling-oriented responses.
       3. Leave the situation unstructured.

22. Which one of the following is NOT a chief function of the group leader?   22.____

    A. Help the individual find a functional place in the group.
    B. Help the individual become aware of the value of the group process
    C. Guide the individual into productive areas for group learning
    D. Persuade the individual to participate in the group activities

23. Certain conditions are desired for effective use of group guidance techniques. These   23.____
    conditions vary with persons and situations but one pair of conditions are said to be
    always desirable, if not essential. Choose the MOST desirable pair from the following.

    A. Groups of small size and heterogeneous characteristics
    B. Groups of small size and homogeneous characteristics
    C. Professional training on the part of guidance personnel and participation on a democratic basis
    D. Willingness of the group leader and democratic attitudes of group members

24. Of the following, the MOST essential characteristic of effective group work is its stress on   24.____

    A. interaction of group members
    B. dissemination of information
    C. discipline and control
    D. economy in instruction

25. Which one of the following is the greatest hindrance to a member in contributing his   25.____
    best to the group?

    A. Inability to discipline himself in the interest of the quality of the group performance
    B. Unwillingness to move along on the problem in the direction formulated by the group
    C. Unwillingness to revise his thinking in the light of the dynamics of the situation
    D. Fear, such as fear of the abilities of others, or that his own meanings will be unacceptable to the group

KEY (CORRECT ANSWERS)

1.	A	11.	D
2.	A	12.	D
3.	B	13.	D
4.	C	14.	B
5.	A	15.	B
6.	D	16.	B
7.	A	17.	D
8.	C	18.	A
9.	C	19.	C
10.	B	20.	A

21. D
22. D
23. C
24. A
25. D

TEST 2

DIRECTIONS: Each question or incomplete statement is followed by several suggested answers or completions. Select the one that BEST answers the question or completes the statement. *PRINT THE LETTER OF THE CORRECT ANSWER IN THE SPACE AT THE RIGHT.*

1. Of the following, the particular value of group guidance lies in the fact that

    A. topics which can be discussed in individual guidance can be discussed more economically in group guidance
    B. group guidance can be conducted by therapists
    C. it is easier to detect children who are emotionally disturbed in group guidance
    D. the group helps children express themselves more freely about common problems

2. Which statement is LEAST true with respect to group-centered counseling?

    A. Group-centered counseling is focused upon personality integration and growth rather than solution of particular problems.
    B. The emphasis is upon the emotional rather than the intellectual aspects of understanding.
    C. The counselor promotes insight directly, using interpretations and recommendations where necessary.
    D. The counselor encourages free expression by recognizing and accepting all expressions without displaying approval or disapproval.

3. In applying the findings of group dynamics to classroom management and learning, which of the following is NOT appropriate?

    A. Create an atmosphere with minimal anxiety and threat.
    B. Clients should be permitted to make the group decisions without the possibility of the therapist's overriding the decisions.
    C. Encourage free discussion and questioning in the classroom.
    D. Lecture methods are less effective devices for obtaining behavioral change than discussion methods.

4. In parent group education discussions, the role of the leader will LEAST likely be to

    A. set the framework for discussion from the members' own experiences
    B. get every member to talk
    C. elicit as many different experiences as possible on any one point in the discussion
    D. help the group move toward its own independent thinking

5. Of the following, the most significant goal in parent group education is to help

    A. isolated parents to socialize
    B. parents better understand their children's needs at different stages of development
    C. parents learn the best techniques for handling children
    D. parents ventilate their guilt feelings

6. In group guidance, the counselor would deal primarily with which of the following needs of students?

   A. Informational and attitudinal
   B. Therapeutic
   C. Informational and therapeutic
   D. Attitudinal and therapeutic

7. When a client in a group guidance session embarks upon a long discourse which is apparently tangential to the main topic under discussion, the leader should

   A. by a gentle reminder bring him back to the main topic before the group censures him
   B. without impatience await reactions from the group
   C. ask another group member if he understands the speaker's message
   D. ask the speaker if he would like to explain to the group his reason for this recountal

8. When a client opens group discussion by voicing extreme hostility against adults, the leader should

   A. interpret his remarks as a frequent reaction of youth
   B. present the adult point of view so there will be a complete picture for reference in further discussion
   C. indicate little interest in his remarks and initiate a more constructive theme
   D. encourage the group to develop the subject

9. Which of the following statements LEAST characterizes the professional parent education discussion group programs?

   A. They represent one of many parent education services.
   B. They draw from many different professional disciplines.
   C. They illustrate one type of group method, specifically defined as to goal, method and organizational structure.
   D. They serve to resolve inner emotional conflicts which parents may have.

10. If the findings of research in group dynamics are applicable to the classroom situation, one would expect clients enrolled in classrooms characterized by a "laissez-faire" approach to find it MOST difficult to

    A. work out plans in advance
    B. evaluate their own progress
    C. attack a new task
    D. make friends

11. The findings of research studies that have contrasted leaders and nonleaders in the same group generally agree that leaders are superior to nonleaders in

    A. intelligence
    B. ability to accept criticism
    C. ability to differentiate right from wrong
    D. intensity of interests

12. Research in group processes has demonstrated that an individual will accept the attitudes of a group if he

    A. is ambitious
    B. rebels against authority
    C. makes friends quickly
    D. is a passive drifter

13. In a group guidance lesson, airing prejudices and counter-prejudices will

    A. promote a willingness on the part of the clients to probe more deeply into the topic
    B. arouse antagonisms that might well have been allowed to be dormant
    C. serve to confuse the pupil by exposing him to conflicting opinions
    D. lead to constructive action by forcing the client to make a choice

14. As contrasted with the class in which activities are group controlled, the class dominated by the therapist

    A. provides little opportunity for social learning
    B. shows less mastery of course material
    C. increases client anxiety and frustration
    D. promotes self-understanding and self-direction

15. Excessive domination of a group of children by an adult leader tends to

    A. increase the cohesiveness of the members of the group
    B. suppress the initiative of the members of the group
    C. increase the awareness of the group members of group goals
    D. prevent the formation of subgroups and cliques

16. Studies of the characteristics of leaders have made it clear that the leader of a group

    A. contributes more to the satisfaction of the needs of the members of the group than any other member
    B. differs from the other members of the group in degree of acceptance of nongroup members
    C. is more concerned with his individual problems than other members of the group
    D. is willing to devote more time and energy to the purpose of the group than any other member

17. SOCIOMETRY IN GROUP RELATIONS was written by

    A. Truda T. Weil   B. Helen Jennings
    C. Frances Wilson   D. Helen Witmer

18. The ability of an individual to persist as the leader of a group depends upon the adaptability of the leader and the

    A. stability of the group structure
    B. size of the group
    C. sex of the group members
    D. socioeconomic level of the group members

19. Of the following, the one that is NOT a prerequisite for the spontaneous formation of a stable group from an aggregate of individuals is

    A. motivation in terms of a common objective
    B. communication among the individuals
    C. mutual acceptance among the prospective members of the group
    D. similarity in social class

20. The degree of cohesiveness that has been established in a group can be increased MOST effectively by

    A. increasing the amount of interaction in the group
    B. modifying the purposes for which the group has been organized
    C. increasing the size of the group
    D. having non-group members criticize the leadership of the group

21. Studies of small groups have indicated that the less cohesive the group, the

    A. less susceptible the group to disruption caused by loss of a leader
    B. more it realizes its lack of solidarity
    C. less strongly will it defend itself against external criticism
    D. less permissive will it be of deviations from group standards

22. After a group has formed and become a cohesive unit, psychologists have defined four additional stages in its development: (a) the group
    I. The group develops its own norms of behavior
    II. The group develops its own "atmosphere"
    III. The status and role of individuals in the group become differentiated.
    IV. Collective goals begin to emerge.
    The sequence in which these four stages generally appear is

    A. I, II, III, IV
    B. II, IV, III, I
    C. III, I, IV, II
    D. IV, III, I, II

23. Which one of the following traits is of most importance in enabling an individual to maintain long-term leadership of a group?

    A. Empathy
    B. Sympathy
    C. Selflessness
    D. Egotism

24. Of the following, group approaches are COMMONLY used for

    A. encounter, discussion, training, and administration
    B. education, counseling, therapy, and recreation
    C. counseling, recreation, catharsis, and crisis intervention
    D. counseling, leadership, administration, and training

25. The purposes of group counseling are the following, with the EXCEPTION of

    A. avoidance of treating pathology as such
    B. helping clients attain a better level of functioning
    C. modifying social and familial problems
    D. resolving intra-psychic conflicts

KEY (CORRECT ANSWERS)

1.	D	11.	A
2.	C	12.	C
3.	B	13.	A
4.	B	14.	A
5.	B	15.	B
6.	A	16.	A
7.	B	17.	B
8.	D	18.	A
9.	D	19.	D
10.	C	20.	A

21. C
22. D
23. A
24. B
25. D

READING COMPREHENSION
UNDERSTANDING AND INTERPRETING WRITTEN MATERIAL
EXAMINATION SECTION
TEST 1

DIRECTIONS: Each question or incomplete statement is followed by several suggested answers or completions. Select the one that BEST answers the question or completes the statement. *PRINT THE LETTER OF THE CORRECT ANSWER IN THE SPACE AT THE RIGHT.*

Questions 1-5.

DIRECTIONS: Questions 1 through 5 are to be answered SOLELY on the basis of the following paragraph.

There are several different schools of thought about the causes of juvenile delinquency. According to the *cultural-transmission* school of thought, delinquency is neither inborn nor developed independently. Children learn to become delinquents as members of groups in which delinquent conduct is already established and *the thing to do*. This school maintains that a child need not be different from other children or have any problems or defects of personality or intelligence in order to become a delinquent. On the other hand, the *psychogenic* school views delinquency as a method of coping with some underlying problem of adjustment. This school also holds that the tendency to become delinquent is not inherited. The delinquent, however, has frustrations, deprivations, insecurities, anxieties, guilt feelings, or mental conflicts which differ in kind or degree from those of non-delinquent children. Delinquency is thought of as a symptom of the underlying problem of adjustment in the same way as a fever is a symptom of an underlying infection. According to this school, if other children exhibit the same behavior, it is because they have independently found a similar solution to their problems.

1. Of the following, the MOST suitable title for the above paragraph would be

    A. PROBLEMS IN THE SCIENTIFIC STUDY OF JUVENILE DELINQUENCY
    B. THE EFFECT OF DISTURBED FAMILY SITUATION
    C. TWO THEORIES OF JUVENILE DELINQUENCY
    D. SOLUTIONS TO A MAJOR SOCIAL PROBLEM

2. According to the above paragraph, the *cultural-transmission* school of thought holds that there is a definite relationship between juvenile delinquency and the youths'

    A. intelligence
    B. psychological problems
    C. family problems
    D. choice of friends

3. According to the above paragraph, of the following, both schools of thought reject as a cause of juvenile delinquency the factor of

    A. guilt feelings
    B. inherited traits
    C. repeated frustration
    D. extreme insecurities

4. On the basis of the above paragraph, which of the following statements is CORRECT?

    A. The *cultural-transmission* school of thought maintains that a child independently develops delinquent behavior as a solution to his problems.
    B. The *psychogenic* school of thought holds that children become delinquents because it is *the thing to do.*
    C. The *cultural-transmission* school of thought maintains that delinquency is the visible symptom of an underlying personality problem.
    D. The *psychogenic* school of thought holds that delinquents have mental conflicts that differ in kind or degree from non-delinquents.

5. The author's attitude toward these schools of thought is that he

    A. describes them objectively without indicating partiality to either school of thought
    B. favors the *cultural-transmission* school of thought
    C. favors the *psychogenic* school of thought
    D. suggests that he thinks both schools of thought are incorrect

Questions 6-7.

DIRECTIONS: Questions 6 and 7 are to be answered SOLELY on the basis of the following paragraph.

Behavior that seems strange to adults often is motivated by the child's desire to please his peers or to gain their attention. His feelings when ridiculed by his peers may range from grief to rage. It is difficult for the child to express such feelings and the reasons for them to adults for to do so he must admit to himself the bitter fact that persons whose friendship he wants really do not like him. Instead of directly expressing his feelings, he may reveal them through symptoms such as fault-finding, fighting back, and complaining. As a result, adults may not realize that when he is telling them how much he dislikes certain children, he may really be expressing how much he would like to be liked by these same children, or how deeply he feels contempt of himself.

6. This paragraph implies that a child's constant complaints about certain other children may be his way of expressing

    A. his desire to be accepted by them
    B. his dislike of the adults around him
    C. ridicule for those he does not like
    D. how many faults those other children have

7. According to the above paragraph, a child may find it difficult to express his grief at being rejected by his peer group because

    A. his rejection motivates him to behave strangely
    B. he knows that the adults around him would not understand his grief
    C. he may not be able to admit the fact of his rejection to himself
    D. his anger prevents him from expressing grief

Questions 8-9.

DIRECTIONS: Questions 8 and 9 are to be answered SOLELY on the basis of the following paragraph.

A very small child has no concept of right or wrong. However, as soon as he is sufficiently developed to be aware of forces outside himself, he will begin to see the advantage of behaving so as to win approval and avoid punishment. If the parents' standard of behavior is presented to the child in a consistent manner, the child will begin to incorporate that standard within himself so that he feels the urge to do what his parents want him to do, whether they are there or not. Furthermore, he will feel uncomfortable doing what he thinks is wrong even if there is no probability of discovery and punishment. If the parents' standard of behavior is NOT consistent, the child may grow up too confused to establish any ideal for himself. We then have a youngster who truly does not know right from wrong. He is in danger of having no firm standard of behavior, no conscience, and no feeling of guilt in defying the established community pattern.

8. The author of the above passage implies that a child whose parents do NOT present him with a consistent standard of behavior

   A. will learn the difference between right and wrong when he is older
   B. may feel no guilt when committing delinquent acts
   C. will feel uncomfortable doing what he thinks is wrong
   D. is likely to establish his own ideal standards

9. The above paragraph implies that when a child feels the urge to do what his parents want him to do, even if they are not present, it means that the child

   A. sees the advantages of behaving so as to avoid punishment
   B. has no concept of right and wrong
   C. has begun to develop a conscience based on his parents' standard of behavior
   D. is afraid that his parents will find out if he misbehaves

Questions 10-13.

DIRECTIONS: Questions 10 through 13 are to be answered SOLELY on the basis of the information in the following passage.

NEW YORK CITY GANGS

City social work agencies and the police have been meeting at City Hall to coordinate efforts to defuse the tensions among teenage groups that they fear could flare into warfare once summer vacations begin. Police intelligence units, with the help of the District Attorneys' offices, are gathering information to identify gangs and their territories. A list of 3,000 gang members has already been assembled, and 110 gangs have been identified. Social workers from various agencies like the Department of Social Services, Neighborhood Youth Corps, and the Youth Board, are out every day developing liaison with groups of juveniles through meetings at schools and recreation centers. Many street workers spend their days seeking to ease the intergang hostility, tracing potentially incendiary rumors, and trying to channel willing gang members into participation in established summer programs. The city's Youth Services Agency plans to spend a million dollars for special summer programs in ten main city areas where gang activity is most firmly entrenched. Five of the *gang neighborhoods* are clustered in an area forming most of southeastern Bronx, and it is here that most of the 110 identified gangs have formed. Special Youth Services programs will also be directed toward the Rockaway section of Queens, Chinatown, Washington Heights, and two neighborhoods in northern Staten Island noted for a lot of motorcycle gang activity. Some of these programs will emphasize sports and recreation, others vocational guidance or neighborhood improvement, but each program will be aimed at benefiting all youngsters in the area. Although none of the money will be spent specifically on gang members, the Youth Services Agency is consulting gang leaders, along with other teenagers, on the projects they would like developed in their area.

10. The above passage states that one of the steps taken by street workers in trying to defuse the tensions among teenage gangs is that of

    A. conducting summer school sessions that will benefit all neighborhood youth
    B. monitoring neighborhood sports competitions between rival gangs
    C. developing liaison with community school boards and parent associations
    D. tracing rumors that could intensify intergang hostilities

11. Based on the information given in the above passage on gangs and New York City's gang members, it is CORRECT to state that

    A. there are no teenage gangs located in Brooklyn
    B. most of the gangs identified by the Police are concentrated in one borough
    C. there is a total of 110 gangs in New York City
    D. only a small percentage of gangs in New York City is in Queens

12. According to the above passage, one IMPORTANT aspect of the program is that

    A. youth gang leaders and other teenagers are involved in the planning
    B. money will be given directly to gang members for use on their projects
    C. only gang members will be allowed to participate in the programs
    D. the parents of gang members will act as youth leaders

13. Various city agencies are cooperating in the attempt to keep the city's youth *cool* during the summer school vacation period.
    The above passage does NOT specifically indicate participation in this project by the

    A. Police Department
    B. District Attorney's Office
    C. Board of Education
    D. Department of Social Services

Questions 14-16.

DIRECTIONS: Questions 14 through 16 are to be answered SOLELY on the basis of the following paragraph.

Drug abuse prevention efforts are only in their beginning stages. Far less is known about how to design programs that successfully counter the seductive effects which drugs have upon the young than about how to build clinics and programs to treat those who have become addicts. The latter can be done with enough dollars, managerial competence, and qualified personnel. The former depends upon such intangibles as community leadership, personal attitudes, and, in the final analysis, individual choices. Given this void in our society's understanding of what it is that makes us so vulnerable to addiction, government must build upon its growing experience to invest wisely in those efforts that offer positive alternatives to drug abuse.

14. The one of the following which is probably the BEST title for the above paragraph is

    A. THE YOUTHFUL DRUG ABUSER
    B. GOVERNMENT'S MANAGEMENT OF DRUG PROGRAMS
    C. A SCIENTIFIC ANALYSIS OF DRUG CURES
    D. THE DIFFICULTY OF DRUG ABUSE PREVENTION

15. According to the above paragraph, treating drug addicts as compared to preventing drug addiction among the young is GENERALLY

    A. *easier,* mainly because there is more public interest in this method
    B. *harder,* mainly because qualified personnel are not readily available
    C. *easier,* mainly because there is more known about how to accomplish this objective
    D. *harder,* mainly because confirmed drug addicts do not give up the habit readily

16. According to the above paragraph, the role of government in dealing with the problem of drug addiction and youth should be to

    A. build larger clinics and develop additional programs for treatment of offenders
    B. help attract youth to behavior which is more desirable than that provided by the drug culture
    C. provide the funds and personnel essential to successful enforcement programs
    D. establish centers for the study and analysis of those factors that make our citizens vulnerable to addiction

Questions 17-20.

DIRECTIONS: Questions 17 through 20 are to be answered SOLELY on the basis of the following paragraph.

Many of our city's most troubled drug addicts are not being reached by the existing treatment programs. They either refuse to enter treatment voluntarily or have dropped out of these programs. A substantial number of the city's heroin addicts, including some of the most crime-prone, are unlikely to be reached by the mere expansion of existing treatment programs.

17. According to the above paragraph, the drug addicts who have dropped out of existing programs

    A. are habitual criminals beyond hope of chance
    B. could be reached by expanding existing programs
    C. include the seriously disturbed
    D. had been compelled to enroll in such programs

18. According to the above paragraph, some drug addicts are not being aided by current treatment efforts because those addicts

    A. are serving excessively long prison sentences
    B. are unwilling to become involved in programs
    C. have been accepted by therapeutic communities
    D. have lost confidence in the city's programs

19. As used in the above paragraph, the underlined word prone means MOST NEARLY

    A. angered   B. bold   C. exclusive   D. inclined

20. As used in the above paragraph, the underlined word mere means MOST NEARLY

    A. formal   B. simple   C. remote   D. prompt

Questions 21-23.

DIRECTIONS: Questions 21 through 23 are to be answered SOLELY on the basis of the following passage.

A survey of the drinking behavior of 1,185 persons representing the adult population of Iowa in 2008 aged 21 years and older revealed that approximately 40 percent were abstainers. Of the nearly one million drinkers in the State, 47 percent were classed as light drinkers, 37 percent as moderate, and 16 percent as heavy drinkers. Twenty-two percent of the men drinkers were classed as heavy drinkers but only 8 percent of the women drinkers. The proportion of heavy drinkers increased with level of education among drinkers residing in the city - from 15 percent of the least educated to 22 percent of the most educated; but decreased among farm residents from 17 percent of the least educated to 4 percent of the most educated. Age differences in the extent of drinking were not pronounced. The age class of 36-45 had the lowest proportions of light drinkers, while the age class 61 and over had the lowest proportion of heavy drinkers.

21. According to the above passage, which one of the following statements concerning heavy drinking would be CORRECT?

    A. Experts are in sharp conflict regarding the reason for heavy drinking.
    B. The amount of heavy drinking in the city is directly proportional to the amount of education.
    C. The degree of heavy drinking is directly proportional to the age class of the drinkers.
    D. The degree of heavy drinking is inversely to the number of light drinkers.

22. Of the total drinking population in Iowa, how many were moderate drinkers?

    A. 370,000   B. 438   C. 370   D. 438,150

23. What percent of the men drinkers surveyed were NOT heavy drinkers?

    A. 60%   B. 84%
    C. 78%   D. Cannot be determined

Questions 24-25.

DIRECTIONS: Questions 24 and 25 are to be answered SOLELY on the basis of the following paragraph.

A drug-user does not completely retreat from society. While a new user, he must begin participation in some group of old users in order to secure access to a steady supply of drugs. In the process, his readiness to engage in drug use, which stems from his personality and the social structure, is reinforced by new patterns of associations and values. The more the individual is caught in this web of associations, the more likely it is that he will persist in drug use, for he has become incorporated into a subculture that exerts control over his behavior. However, it is also true that the resulting tics among addicts are not as strong as those among participants in criminal and conflict subcultures. Addiction is in many ways an individualistic adaptation for the *kick* is essentially a private experience. The compelling need for the drug is also a divisive force for it leads to intense competition among addicts for money. Forces of this kind thus limit the relative cohesion which can develop among users.

24. According to the above paragraph, the MAIN reason why new drug users associate with old users is a   24._____

    A. fear of the police
    B. common hatred of society
    C. need to get drugs
    D. dislike of being alone

25. According to the above paragraph, which of the following statements is INCORRECT?   25._____

    A. Drug users encourage each other to continue taking drugs.
    B. Gangs that use drugs are more cohesive than other delinquent gangs.
    C. A youth's desire to use drugs stems from his personality as well as the social structure.
    D. Addicts get no more of a *kick* from using drugs in a group than alone.

KEY (CORRECT ANSWERS)

1. C
2. D
3. B
4. D
5. A

6. A
7. C
8. B
9. C
10. D

11. B
12. A
13. C
14. D
15. C

16. B
17. C
18. B
19. D
20. B

21. B
22. A
23. C
24. C
25. B

TEST 2

DIRECTIONS: Each question or incomplete statement is followed by several suggested answers or completions. Select the one that BEST answers the question or completes the statement. *PRINT THE LETTER OF THE CORRECT ANSWER IN THE SPACE AT THE RIGHT.*

Questions 1-5.

DIRECTIONS: Questions 1 through 5 are to be answered SOLELY on the basis of the following passage.

In an attempt to describe what is meant by a delinquent subculture, let us look at some delinquent activities. We usually assume that when people steal things, they steal because they want them to eat or wear or otherwise use them; or because they can sell them; or even –if we are given to a psychoanalytic turn of mind–because on some deep symbolic level the things stolen substitute or stand for something unconsciously desired but forbidden. However, most delinquent gang stealing has no such utilitarian motivation at all. Even where the value of the object stolen is itself a motivating consideration, the stolen sweets are often sweeter than those acquired by more legitimate and prosaic means. In homelier language, stealing *for the hell of it* and apart from considerations of gain and profit is a valued activity to which attaches glory, prowess, and profound satisfaction.

Similarly, many other delinquent activities are motivated mainly by an enjoyment in the distress of others and by a hostility toward non-gang peers as well as adults. Apart from the more dramatic manifestations in the form of gang wars, there is keen delight in terrorizing *good* children and in driving them from playgrounds and gyms for which the gang itself may have little use. The same spirit is evident in playing hooky and in misbehavior in school. The teacher and her rules are not merely to be evaded. They are to be flouted.

All this suggests that the delinquent subculture is not only a set of rules, a design for living which is different from or indifferent to or even in conflict with the norms of the *respectable* adult society. It actually takes its norms from the larger culture but turns them upside down. The delinquent's conduct is right, by the standards of his subculture, precisely BECAUSE it is wrong by the standards of the larger culture.

1. Of the following, the MOST suitable title for the above passage is

    A. DIFFERENT KINDS OF DELINQUENT SUBCULTURES
    B. DELINQUENT HOSTILITY TOWARD NON-GANG PEERS
    C. METHODS OF DELINQUENT STEALING
    D. DELINQUENT STANDARDS AS REVEALED BY THEIR ACTIVITIES

2. It may be inferred from the above passage that MOST delinquent stealing is motivated by a

    A. need for food and clothing
    B. need for money to buy drugs
    C. desire for peer-approval
    D. symbolic identification of the thing stolen with hidden desires

3. The passage IMPLIES that an important reason why delinquents play hooky and misbehave in school is that the teachers

   A. represent *respectable* society
   B. are boring
   C. have not taught them the values of the adult society
   D. are too demanding

4. In the above passage, the author's attitude toward delinquents is

   A. critical   B. objective
   C. overly sympathetic   D. confused

5. According to the above passage, which of the following statements is CORRECT?

   A. Delinquents derive no satisfaction from stealing.
   B. Delinquents are not hostile toward someone without a reason.
   C. The common motive of many delinquent activities is a desire to frustrate others.
   D. The delinquent subculture shares its standards with the *respectable* adult culture.

Questions 6-8.

DIRECTIONS: Questions 6 through 8 are to be answered SOLELY on the basis of the following paragraph.

A fundamental part of the youth worker's role is changing the interaction patterns which already exist between the delinquent group and the representatives of key institutions in the community; e.g., the policeman, teacher, social worker, employer, parent, and storekeeper. This relationship, particularly its definitional character, is a two-way proposition. The offending youth or group will usually respond by fulfilling this prophecy. In the same way, the delinquent expects punishment or antagonistic treatment from officials and other representatives of middle class society. In turn, the adult concerned may act to fulfill the prophecy of the delinquent. Stereotyped patterns of expectation, both of the delinquents and those in contact with them, must be changed. The worker can be instrumental in changing these patterns.

6. Of the following, the MOST suitable title for the above paragraph is

   A. WAYS TO PREDICT JUVENILE DELINQUENCY
   B. THE YOUTH WORKER'S ROLE IN CREATING STEREOTYPES
   C. THE YOUTH WORKER'S ROLE IN CHANGING STEREOTYPED PATTERNS OF EXPECTATION
   D. THE DESIRABILITY OF INTERACTION PATTERNS

7. According to the above paragraph, a youth who misbehaves and is told by an agency worker that *his group is a menace to the community* would PROBABLY eventually respond by

   A. withdrawing into himself
   B. continuing to misbehave
   C. making a greater attempt to please
   D. acting indifferent

8. In the above paragraph, the author's opinion about stereotypes is that they are

A. *useful,* primarily because they are usually accurate
B. *useful,* primarily because they make a quick response easier
C. *harmful,* primarily because the adult community will be less aware of delinquents as a group
D. *harmful,* primarily because they influence behavior

Questions 9-15.

DIRECTIONS: Questions 9 through 15 are to be answered SOLELY on the basis of the information in the following passage.

Laws concerning juveniles make it clear that the function of the courts is to treat delinquents, not to punish them. Many years ago, children were detained in jails or police lockups along with adult offenders. Today, however, it is recognized that separate detention is important for the protection of the children. Detention is now regarded as part of the treatment process.

Detention is not an ordinary child care job. On the one hand, it must be distinguished from mere shelter care, which is a custodial program for children whose families cannot care for them adequately. On the other hand, it must be distinguished from treatment in mental health institutions, which is meant for children who have very serious mental or psychological problems. The children in a detention facility are there because they have run into trouble with the law and because they must be kept in safe custody for a short period until the court decides the final action to be taken in each child's case.

The Advisory Committee on Detention and Shelter Care has outlined several basic objectives for a good detention service. One objective is secure custody. Like adults who are being detained until their cases come up before the court, children too will often want to escape from detention. Security measures must be adequate to prevent ordinary escape attempts, although at the same time a jail-like atmosphere should be avoided. Another objective is to provide constructive activities for the children and to give individual guidance through casework and group sessions. A final objective is to study each child individually so that useful information can be provided for court action and so that the mental, emotional, or other problems that have contributed to the child's difficulties can be identified.

9. According to the above passage, laws concerning juveniles make it clear that the MAIN aim of the courts in handling young offenders is to _____ juvenile delinquents.

   A. punish
   B. provide treatment for
   C. relieve the families of
   D. counsel families which have

10. The above passage IMPLIES that the former practice of locking up juveniles along with adults was

   A. *good* because it was more efficient than providing separate facilities
   B. *good* because children could then be protected by the adults
   C. *bad* because the children were not safe
   D. *bad* because delinquents need mental health treatment

11. The above passage says that a detention center differs from a shelter care facility in that the children in a detention center

    A. have been placed there permanently by their families or by the courts
    B. come from families who cannot or will not care for them
    C. have serious mental or psychological problems
    D. are in trouble with the law and must be kept in safe custody temporarily

12. The above passage mentions one specific way in which detained juveniles are like detained adults.
    This similarity is that both detained juveniles and detained adults

    A. may try to escape from the detention facility
    B. have been convicted of serious crimes
    C. usually come from bad family backgrounds
    D. have mental or emotional problems

13. The above passage lists several basic objectives that were outlined by the Advisory Committee on Detention and Child Care.
    Which one of the following aims is NOT given in the list of Advisory Committee objectives?

    A. Separating juvenile offenders from adult offenders
    B. Providing secure custody
    C. Giving individual guidance
    D. Providing useful information for court action

14. The above passage mentions a *custodial program*. This means MOST NEARLY

    A. janitor services
    B. a program to prevent jail escapes
    C. caretaking services for dependent children
    D. welfare payments to families with children

15. The above passage says that *security measures* are needed in a detention center PRIMARILY in order to

    A. prevent unauthorized persons from entering
    B. prevent juveniles from escaping
    C. ensure that records are safeguarded for court action
    D. create a jail-like atmosphere

Questions 16-22.

DIRECTIONS: Questions 16 through 22 are to be answered SOLELY on the basis of the following passage.

Adolescents are among the last social groups in the world to be given the full nineteenth-century colonial treatment. Our colonial administrators, at least at the higher policymaking levels, are usually of the enlightened sort who decry the punitive expedition except as an instrument of last resort, though they are inclined to tolerate a shade more brutality in the actual school or police station than the law allows. They prefer, however, to study the young with a view to understanding them, not for their own sake but in order to learn how to induce them to abandon their barbarism and assimilate the folkways of normal adult life. The model emissary to the world of youth is no longer the tough disciplinarian but the trained youth worker, who works like a psychoanalytically oriented anthropologist. Like the best of missionaries, he is sent to work with, and is aware and critical of the larger society he represents. But fundamentally, he accepts it and often does not really question its basic value or its right to send him to wean the young from savagery.

The economic position of *the adolescent society,* like that of other colonies, is highly ambiguous. It is simultaneously a costly drain on the commonwealth and a vested interest of those members of the commonwealth who earn their living and their social role by exploiting it. Juvenile delinquency is destructive and wasteful, and efforts to control and combat it are expensive. Schooling is even more expensive. Both undertakings are justified on the assumption that youth must be drawn into the social order if the social order is to continue, and this is self-evident. But both act as agents of society as it now is, propagating social values and assumptions among a youth often cynical and distrustful but ignorant of the language or the moral judgments in terms of which social complaints might be couched. Neither the youth agency nor the school is usually competent or sufficiently independent to help adolescents examine the sources of their pain and conflict and think its meaning through, using their continuing experience of life to help them build better social arrangements in their turn. This, in a democracy, ought clearly to be among the most fundamental functions of citizenship education; in a public school system geared and responsive to local political demands and interests, it may well be impossible. Official agencies dealing with youth vary enormously in the pretexts and techniques with which they approach their clientele, from those of the young worker attached to a conflict gang to those of the citizenship education teacher in the academic track of a suburban high school. But they all begin, like a Colonial Office, with the assumption that the long-term interests of their clientele are consistent with the present interests of their sponsor.

16. The clientele and sponsor of official agencies dealing with youth are the

    A. young and the adult
    B. young and the educators
    C. educators and the young
    D. adult and the middle class

17. The author believes that the adolescent society is

    A. a drain on the commonwealth from which almost no one benefits
    B. the mainstay of the economy
    C. mercilessly exploited by certain adults
    D. costly to the government but a financial boon to certain adults

18. The author feels that society's present attempts to assimilate youth are motivated by

    A. greed
    B. a desire to end juvenile delinquency
    C. a desire to maintain the status quo
    D. a desire to induce the young to abandon their barbarism

19. The author is _____ society and _____ of youth.

    A. *approving* of present day; disapproving
    B. *approving* of present day; approving
    C. *disapproving* of adult; disapproving
    D. *disapproving* of adult; approving

20. According to the above passage, the BASIC function of citizenship education in a democracy ought to be to 20._____

   A. help adolescents examine the source of their pain and conflict
   B. help adolescents think the meaning of their problems through
   C. enable adolescents to perceive the meaning of experience
   D. enable adolescents to improve society through an understanding of their problems

21. The author is LEAST critical of 21._____

   A. nineteenth-century Colonialists
   B. the trained youth worker
   C. the members of the commonwealth who earn their living exploiting youth
   D. official agencies dealing with youth

22. It is implied in the above passage that 22._____

   A. colonialism is beneficial to the colonies
   B. society should not be stagnant but needs change
   C. society should have more effective ways of disciplining recidivists
   D. youth is more interested in track than citizenship education

Question 23.

DIRECTIONS: Question 23 is to be answered SOLELY on the basis of the following passage.

Some adolescents find it very difficult to take the first step toward independence. Instead of experimenting as his friends do, a teenager may stay close to home, conforming to his parents' wishes. Sometimes parents and school authorities regard this untroublesome youngster with satisfaction and admiration, but they are wrong to do so. A too-conforming adolescent will not develop into an independent adult.

23. The above passage implies that a teenager who always conforms to his parents' wishes 23._____

   A. should be admired by his teachers
   B. will develop into a troublesome person
   C. will become very independent
   D. should be encouraged to act more independently

Questions 24-25.

DIRECTIONS: Questions 24 and 25 are to be answered SOLELY on the basis of the following paragraph.

The skilled children's counselor can encourage the handicapped child to make a maximum adjustment to the demands of learning and socialization. She will be aware that the child's needs are basically the same as those of other children and yet she will be sensitive to his special needs and the ways in which these are met. She will understand the frustration the child may experience when he cannot participate in the simple activities of childhood. She will also be aware of the need to help him to avoid repeated failures by encouraging him to engage in projects in which he can generally succeed and perhaps excel.

24. According to the above paragraph, it is important for the children's counselor to realize that the handicapped child

   A. should not participate in ordinary activities
   B. must not be treated in any special way
   C. is sensitive to the counselor's problems
   D. has needs similar to those of other children

25. According to the above paragraph, the counselor can BEST help the handicapped child to avoid frustrating situations by encouraging him to

   A. participate in the same activities as *normal* children
   B. participate in activities which are not too difficult for him
   C. engage in projects which are interesting
   D. excel in difficult games

KEY (CORRECT ANSWERS)

1.	D	11.	D
2.	C	12.	A
3.	A	13.	A
4.	B	14.	C
5.	C	15.	B
6.	C	16.	A
7.	B	17.	D
8.	D	18.	C
9.	B	19.	D
10.	C	20.	D

21. B
22. B
23. D
24. D
25. B

REPORT WRITING

EXAMINATION SECTION

TEST 1

DIRECTIONS: Each question or incomplete statement is followed by several suggested answers or completions. Select the one that BEST answers the question or completes the statement. *PRINT THE LETTER OF THE CORRECT ANSWER IN THE SPACE AT THE RIGHT.*

Questions 1-3.

DIRECTIONS: Questions 1 to 3 are based on the following example of a report. The report consists of ten numbered sentences, some of which are *not* consistent with the principles of good report writing.

(1) On the evening of February 24, Roscoe and Leroy, two members of the "Red Devils," were entering with a bottle of wine in their hands. (2) It was unusually good wine for these boys to buy, (3) I told them to give me the bottle and they refused, and added that they wouldn't let anyone "put them out." (4) I told them they were entitled to have a good time, but they could not do it the way they wanted; there were certain rules they had to observe. (5) At this point, Roscoe said he had seen me box at camp and suggested that Leroy not accept my offer. (6) Then I said firmly that the admission fee did not give them the authority to tell me what to do. (7) I also told them that, if they thought I would fight them over such a matter, they were sadly mistaken. (8) I added, however, that we could go to the gym right now and settle it another way if they wished. (9) Leroy immediately said that he was sorry, he had not understood the rules, and he did not want his quarter back. (10) On the other hand, they would not give up their bottle either, so they left the premises.

1. Only material that is relevant to the main thought of a report should be included. Which of the following sentences from the report contains material which is LEAST relevant to this report? Sentence
   "A. 2   B. 3   C. 8   D. 9

2. A good report should be arranged in logical order. Which of the following sentences from the report does NOT appear in its proper sequence in the report? Sentence
   A. 3   B. 5   C. 7   D. 9

3. Reports should include all essential information. Of the following, the MOST important fact that is *missing* from this report is:
   A. Who was involved in the incident   B. How the incident was resolved
   C. When the incident took place   D. Where the incident took place

4. The MOST serious of the following faults *commonly* found in explanatory reports is
   A. the use of slang terms   B. excessive details
   C. personal bias   D. redundancy

5. In reviewing a report he has prepared to submit to his superiors, a supervisor finds that his paragraphs are a typewritten page long and decides to make some revisions.
Of the following, the MOST important question he should ask about each paragraph is
   A. Are the words too lengthy?
   B. Is the idea under discussion too abstract?
   C. Is more than one central thought being expressed?
   D. Are the sentences too long?

5.____

6. The summary or findings of a long management report intended for the typical manager should, *generally*, appear _____ the report.
   A. at the very beginning of
   B. at the end of
   C. throughout
   D. in the middle of

6.____

7. In preparing a report that includes several tables, if not otherwise instructed, the typist should MOST properly include a list of tables
   A. in the introductory part of the report
   B. at the end of each chapter in the body of the report
   C. in the supplementary part of the report as an appendix
   D. in the supplementary part of the report as a part of the index

7.____

8. When typing a preliminary draft of a report, the one of the following which you should *generally* NOT do is to
   A. erase typing errors and deletions rather than "X"ing them out
   B. leave plenty of room at the top, bottom, and sides of each page
   C. make only the number of copies that you are asked to make
   D. type double or triple space

8.____

9. When you determine the methods of emphasis you will use in typing the titles, headings and subheadings of a report, the one of the following which it is MOST important to keep in mind is that
   A. all headings of the same rank should be typed in the same way
   B. all headings should be typed in the single style which is most pleasing to the eye
   C. headings should not take up more than one-third of the page width
   D. only one method should be used for all headings, whatever their rank

9.____

10. The one of the following ways in which inter-office memoranda *differ* from long formal reports is that they, *generally*,
    A. are written as if the reader is familiar with the vocabulary and technical background of the writer
    B. do not have a "subject line" which describes the major topic covered in the text
    C. include a listing of reference materials which support the memo writer's conclusions
    D. require that a letter of transmittal be attached

10.____

11. It is *preferable* to print information on a field report rather than write it out longhand MAINLY because
    A. printing takes less time to write than writing long hand
    B. printing is usually easier to read than longhand writing
    C. longhand writing on field reports is not acceptable in court cases
    D. printing occupies less space on a report than longhand writing

12. Of the following characteristics of a written report, the one that is MOST important is its
    A. length   B. accuracy   C. organization   D. grammar

13. A written report to your superior contains many spelling errors.
    Of the following statements relating to spelling errors, the one that is MOST NEARLY correct is that
    A. this is unimportant as long as the meaning of the report is clear
    B. readers of the report will ignore the many spelling errors
    C. readers of the report will get a poor opinion of the writer of the report
    D. spelling errors are unimportant as long as the grammar is correct

14. Written reports to your superior should have the same general arrangement and layout.
    The BEST reason for this requirement is that the
    A. report will be more accurate
    B. report will be more complete
    C. person who reads the report will know what the subject of the report is
    D. person who reads the report will know where to look for information in the report

15. The first paragraph of a report usually contains detailed information on the subject of the report.
    Of the following, the BEST reason for this requirement is to enable the
    A. reader to quickly find the subject of the report
    B. typist to immediately determine the subject of the report so that she will understand what she is typing
    C. clerk to determine to whom copies of the report will be needed
    D. typist to quickly determine how many copies of the report will be needed

16. Of the following statements concerning reports, the one which is LEAST valid is:
    A. A case report should contain factual material to support conclusions made
    B. An extremely detailed report may be of less value than a brief report giving the essential facts
    C. Highly technical language should be avoided as far as possible in preparing a report to be used at a court trial
    D. The position of the important facts in a report does not influence the emphasis placed on them by the reader

17. Suppose that you realize that you have made an error in a report that has been forwarded to another unit. You know that this error is not likely to be discovered for some time.
Of the following, the MOST advisable course of action for you to take is to
   A. approach the supervisor of the other unit on an informal basis, and ask him to correct the error
   B. say nothing about it since most likely one error will not invalidate the entire report
   C. tell your supervisor immediately that you have made an error so that it may be corrected, if necessary
   D. wait until the error is discovered and then admit that you had made it

17._____

18. In a report, words in a sentence must be arranged properly to make sure that the intended meaning of the sentence is clear.
The sentence below that does NOT make sense because a clause has been separated from the word on which its meaning depends is:
   A. To be a good writer, clarity is necessary.
   B. To be a good writer, you must write clearly.
   C. You must write clearly to be a good writer.
   D. Clarity is necessary to good writing.

18._____

19. The use of a graph to show statistical data in a report is *superior* to a table because it
   A. emphasizes approximations
   B. emphasizes facts and relationships more dramatically
   C. presents data more accurately
   D. is easily understood by the average reader

19._____

20. Of the following, the degree of formality required of a written report is, MOST likely to depend on the
   A. subject matter of the report
   B. frequency of its occurrence
   C. amount of time available for its preparation
   D. audience for whom the report is intended

20._____

Questions 21-25.

DIRECTIONS: Questions 21 through 25 consist of sets of four sentences lettered A, B, C, and D. For each question, choose the sentence which is grammatically and stylistically MOST appropriate for use in a formal written report.

21. A. It is recommended, therefore, that the impasse panel hearings are to be convened on September 30.
    B. It is therefore recommended that the impasse panel hearings be convened on September 30.
    C. Therefore, it is recommended to convene the impasse panel hearings on September 30.
    D. It is recommended that the impasse panel hearings therefore should be convened on September 30.

21._____

5 (#1)

22.　A.　Penalties have been assessed for violating the Taylor Law by several unions. 22.____
　　B.　When they violated provisions of the Taylor Law, several unions were later penalized.
　　C.　Several unions have been penalized for violating provisions of the Taylor Law.
　　D.　Several unions' violating provisions of the Taylor Law resulted in them being penalized.

23.　A.　The number of disputes settled through mediation has increased significantly over the past two years. 23.____
　　B.　The number of disputes settled through mediation are increasing significantly over two-year periods.
　　C.　Over the past two years, through mediation, the number of disputes settled increased significantly.
　　D.　There is a significant increase over the past two years of the number of disputes settled through mediation.

24.　A.　The union members will vote to determine if the contract is to be approved. 24.____
　　B.　It is not yet known whether the union members will ratify the proposed contract.
　　C.　When the union members vote, that will determine the new contract.
　　D.　Whether the union members will ratify the proposed contract, it is not yet known.

25.　A.　The parties agreed to an increase in fringe benefits in return for greater work productivity. 25.____
　　B.　Greater productivity was agreed to be provided in return for increased fringe benefits.
　　C.　Productivity and fringe benefits are interrelated; the higher the former, the more the latter grows.
　　D.　The contract now provides that the amount of fringe benefits will depend upon the level of output by the workers.

KEY (CORRECT ANSWERS)

1.	A	11.	B
2.	B	12.	B
3.	D	13.	C
4.	C	14.	D
5.	C	15.	A
6.	A	16.	D
7.	A	17.	C
8.	A	18.	A
9.	A	19.	B
10.	A	20.	D

21.	B
22.	C
23.	A
24.	B
25.	A

TEST 2

DIRECTIONS: Each question or incomplete statement is followed by several suggested answers or completions. Select the one that BEST answers the question or completes the statement. *PRINT THE LETTER OF THE CORRECT ANSWER IN THE SPACE AT THE RIGHT.*

Questions 1-4.

DIRECTIONS: Questions 1 through 4 are to be answered on the basis of the following report which was prepared by a supervisor for inclusion in his agency's annual report.

Line #

1   On Oct. 13, I was assigned to study the salaries paid
2   to clerical employees in various titles by the city and by
3   private industry in the area.
4   In order to get the data I needed, I called Mr. Johnson at
5   the Bureau of the Budget and the payroll officers at X Corp.-
6   a brokerage house, Y Co. –an insurance company, and Z Inc. –
7   a publishing firm. None of them was available and I had to call
8   all of them again the next day.
9   When I finally got the information I needed, I drew up a
10 chart, which is attached. Note that not all of the companies I
11 contacted employed people at all the different levels used in the
12 city service.
13 The conclusions I draw from analyzing this information is
14 as follows: The city's entry-level salary is about average for
15 the region; middle-level salaries are generally higher in the
16 city government than in private industry; but salaries at the
17 highest levels in private industry are better than city em-
18 ployees' pay.

1. Which of the following criticisms about the style in which this report is written is MOST valid?
   A. It is too informal.
   B. It is too concise.
   C. It is too choppy.
   D. The syntax is too complex.

   1.____

2. Judging from the statements made in the report, the method followed by this employee in performing his research was
   A. *good*; he contacted a representative sample of businesses in the area
   B. *poor*; he should have drawn more definite conclusions
   C. *good*; he was persistent in collecting information
   D. *poor*; he did not make a thorough study

   2.____

3. One sentence in this report contains a grammatical error. This sentence *begins* on line number
   A. 4   B. 7   C. 10   D. 13

   3.____

4. The type of information given in this report which should be presented in footnotes or in an appendix, is the
   A. purpose of the study
   B. specifics about the businesses contacted
   C. reference to the chart
   D. conclusions drawn by the author

5. Of the following, a DISTINGUISHING characteristic of a written report intended for the head of your agency as compared to a report prepared for a lower-echilon staff member is that the report for the agency head should, *usually*, include
   A. considerably more detail, especially statistical data
   B. the essential details in an abbreviated form
   C. all available source material
   D. an annotated bibliography

6. Assume that you are asked to write a lengthy report for use by the administrator of your agency, the subject of which is "The Impact of Proposed New Data Processing Operations on Line Personnel" in your agency. You decide that the *most* appropriate type of report for you to prepare is an analytical report, including recommendations.
   The MAIN reason for your decision is that
   A. the subject of the report is extremely complex
   B. large sums of money are involved
   C. the report is being prepared for the administrator
   D. you intend to include charts and graphs

7. Assume that you are preparing a report based on a survey dealing with the attitudes of employees in Division X regarding proposed new changes in compensating employees for working overtime. Three percent of the respondents to the survey voluntarily offer an unfavorable opinion on the method of assigning overtime work, a question not specifically asked of the employees. On the basis of this information, the MOST appropriate and significant of the following comments for you to make in the report with regard to employees' attitudes on assigning overtime work is that
   A. an insignificant percentage of employees dislike the method of assigning overtime work
   B. three percent of the employees in Division X dislike the method of assigning overtime work
   C. three percent of the sample selected for the survey voiced an unfavorable opinion on the method of assigning overtime work
   D. some employees voluntarily voiced negative feelings about the method of assigning overtime work, making it impossible to determine the extent of this attitude

8. Assume that you have been asked to prepare a narrative summary of the monthly reports submitted by employees in your division.
   In preparing your summary of this month's reports, the FIRST step to take is to
   A. read through the reports, noting their general content and any unusual features
   B. decide how many typewritten pages your summary should contain
   C. make a written summary of each separate report, so that you will not have to go back to the original reports again
   D. ask each employee which points he would prefer to see emphasized in your summary

   8.____

9. Assume that an administrative officer is writing a brief report to his superior outlining the advantages of matrix organization.
   Of the following, it would be INCORRECT to state that
   A. in matrix organization, a project is emphasized by designating one individual as the focal point for all matters pertaining to it
   B. utilization of manpower can be flexible in matrix organization because reservoir of specialists is maintained in the line operations
   C. the usual line-staff management is generally reversed in matrix organization
   D. in matrix organization, responsiveness to project needs is generally faster due to establishing needed communication lines and decision points

   9.____

10. Written reports dealing with inspections of work and installations SHOULD be
    A. as long and detailed as practicable
    B. phrased with personal interpretations
    C. limited to the important facts of the inspection
    D. technically phrased to create an impression on superiors

    10.____

11. It is important to use definite, exact words in preparing a descriptive report and to avoid, as much as possible, nouns that have vague meanings and, possibly, a different meaning for the reader than for the author.
    Which of the following sentences contains only nouns that are *definite* and *exact*?
    A. The free enterprise system should be vigorously encouraged in the United States.
    B. Arley Swopes climbed Mount Everest three times last year.
    C. Beauty is a characteristic of all the women at the party.
    D. Gil Noble asserts that he is a real democrat.

    11.____

12. One way of shortening n unnecessarily long report is to reduce sentence length by eliminating the use of several words where a single one that does not alter the meaning will do.
    Which of the following sentences CANNOT be shortened without losing some of its information content?
    A. After being polished, the steel ball bearings ran at maximum speed.
    B. After the close of the war, John Taylor was made the recipient of a pension.
    C. In this day and age, you can call anyone up on the telephone.
    D. She is attractive in appearance, but she is a rather selfish person.

    12.____

13. Employees are required to submit written reports of all unusual occurrences promptly.
    The BEST reason for such promptness is that the
    A. report may be too long if made at one's convenience
    C. report will tend to be more accurate as to facts
    D. employee is likely to make a better report under pressure

14. In making a report, it is poor practice to erase information on the report in order to make a change because
    A. there may be a question of what was changed and why it was changed
    B. you are likely to erase through the paper and tear the report
    C. the report will no longer look neat and presentable
    D. the duplicate copies will be smudged

15. The one of the following which BEST describes a periodic report is that it
    A. provides a record of accomplishments for a given time span and a comparison with similar time spans in the past
    B. covers the progress made in a project that has been postponed
    C. integrates, summarizes, and, perhaps, interprets published data on technical or scientific material
    D. describes a decision, advocates a policy or action, and presents facts in support of the writer's position

16. The PRIMARY purpose of including pictorial illustrations in a formal report is *usually* to
    A. amplify information which has been adequately treated verbally
    B. present details that are difficult to describe verbally
    C. provide the reader with a pleasant, momentary distraction
    D. present supplementary information incidental to the main ideas developed in the report

KEY (CORRECT ANSWERS)

1.	A		6.	A
2.	D		7.	D
3.	D		8.	A
4.	B		9.	C
5.	B		10.	C

11. B.
12. A.
13. C
14. A.
15. A.
16 B.

PREPARING WRITTEN MATERIAL

PARAGRAPH REARRANGEMENT
COMMENTARY

The sentences that follow are in scrambled order. You are to rearrange them in proper order and indicate the letter choice containing the correct answer at the space at the right.

Each group of sentences in this section is actually a paragraph presented in scrambled order. Each sentence in the group has a place in that paragraph; no sentence is to be left out. You are to read each group of sentences and decide upon the best order in which to put the sentences so as to form a well-organized paragraph.

The questions in this section measure the ability to solve a problem when all the facts relevant to its solution are not given.

More specifically, certain positions of responsibility and authority require the employee to discover connection between events sometimes, apparently, unrelated. In order to do this, the employee will find it necessary to correctly infer that unspecified events have probably occurred or are likely to occur. This ability becomes especially important when action must be taken on incomplete information.

Accordingly, these questions require competitors to choose among several suggested alternatives, each of which presents a different sequential arrangement of the events. Competitors must choose the MOST logical of the suggested sequences.

In order to do so, they may be required to draw on general knowledge to infer missing concepts or events that are essential to sequencing the given events. Competitors should be careful to infer only what is essential to the sequence. The plausibility of the wrong alternatives will always require the inclusion of unlikely events or of additional chains of events which are NOT essential to sequencing the given events.

It's very important to remember that you are looking for the best of the four possible choices, and that the best choice of all may not even be one of the answers you're given to choose from.

There is no one right way to solve these problems. Many people have found it helpful to first write out the order of the sentences, as they would have arranged them, on their scrap paper before looking at the possible answers. If their optimum answer is there, this can save them some time. If it isn't, this method can still give insight into solving the problem. Others find it most helpful to just go through each of the possible choices, contrasting each as they go along. You should use whatever method feels comfortable and works for you.

While most of these types of questions are not that difficult, we've added a higher percentage of the difficult type, just to give you more practice. Usually there are only one or two questions on this section that contain such subtle distinctions that you're unable to answer confidently. And you then may find yourself stuck deciding between two possible choices, neither of which you're sure about.

EXAMINATION SECTION
TEST 1

DIRECTIONS: Each question consists of several sentences which can be arranged in a logical sequence. For each question, select the choice which places the numbered sentences in the MOST logical sequence. *PRINT THE LETTER OF THE CORRECT ANSWER IN THE SPACE AT THE RIGHT.*

1.   I. A body was found in the woods.
    II. A man proclaimed innocence.
    III. The owner of a gun was located.
    IV. A gun was traced.
    V. The owner of a gun was questioned.
    The CORRECT answer is:
    A. IV, III, V, II, I   B. II, I, IV, III, V   C. I, IV, III, V, II
    D. I, III, V, II, IV   E. I, II, IV, III, V

1.____

2.   I. A man is in a hunting accident.
    II. A man fell down a flight of steps.
    III. A man lost his vision in one eye,
    IV. A man broke his leg.
    V. A man had to walk with a cane.
    The CORRECT answer is:
    A. II, IV, V, I, III   B. IV, V, I, III, II   C. III, I, IV, V, II
    D. I, III, V, II, IV   E. I, III, II, IV, V

2.____

3.   I. A man is offered a new job.
    II. A woman is offered a new job.
    III. A man works as a waiter.
    IV. A woman works as a waitress.
    V. A woman gives notice.
    The CORRECT answer is:
    A. IV, II, V, III, I   B. IV, II, V, I, III   C. II, IV, V, III, I
    D. III, I, IV, II, V   E. IV, III, II, V, I

3.____

4.   I. A train let the station late.
    II. A man was late for work.
    III. A man lost his job.
    IV. Many people complained because the train was late.
    V. There was a traffic jam.
    The CORRECT answer is:
    A. V, II, I, IV, III   B. V, I, IV, II, III   C. V, I, II, IV, III
    D. I, V, IV, II, III   E. II, I, IV, V, III

4.____

5.
   I. The burden of proof as to each issue is determined before trial and remains upon the same party throughout the trial.
   II. The jury is at liberty to believe one witness' testimony as against a number of contradictory witnesses.
   III. In a civil case, the party bearing the burden of proof is required to prove his contention by a fair preponderance of the evidence.
   IV. However, it must be noted that a fair preponderance of evidence does not necessarily mean a greater number of witnesses.
   V. The burden of proof is the burden which rests upon one of the parties to an action to persuade the trier of the facts, generally the jury, that a proposition he asserts is true.
   VI. If the evidence is equally balanced, or if it leaves the jury in such doubt as to be unable to decide the controversy either way, judgment must be given against the party upon whom the burden of proof rests.
   The CORRECT answer is:
   A. III. II, V, IV, I, VI   B. I, II, VI, V, III, IV   C. III, IV, V, I, II, VI
   D. V, I, III, VI, IV, II   E. I, V, III, VI, IV, II

6.
   I. If a parent is without assets and is unemployed, he cannot be convicted of the crime of non-support of a child.
   II. The term *sufficient ability* has been held to mean sufficient financial ability.
   III. It does not matter if his unemployment is by choice or unavoidable circumstances.
   IV. If he fails to take any steps at all, he may be liable to prosecution for endangering the welfare of a child.
   V. Under the penal law, a parent is responsible for the support of his minor child only if the parent is of *sufficient ability*.
   VI. An indigent parent may meet his obligation by borrowing money or by seeking aid under the provisions of the Social Welfare Law.
   The CORRECT answer is:
   A. VI, I, V, III, II, IV   B. I, III, V, II, IV, VI   C. V, II, I, III, VI, IV
   D. I, VI, IV, V, II, III   E. II, V, I, III, VI, IV

7.
   I. Consider, for example, the case of a rabble rouser who urges a group of twenty people to go out and break the windows of a nearby factory.
   II. Therefore, the law fills the indicated gap with the crime of *inciting to riot*.
   III. A person is considered guilty of inciting to riot when he urges ten or more persons to engage in tumultuous and violent conduct of a kind likely to create public alarm.
   IV. However, if he has not obtained the cooperation of at least four people, he cannot be charged with unlawful assembly.
   V. The charge of inciting to riot was added to the law to cover types of conduct which cannot be classified as either the crime of *riot* or the crime of *unlawful assembly*.
   VI. If he acquires the acquiescence of at least four of them, he is guilty of unlawful assembly even if the project does not materialize.
   The CORRECT answer is:
   A. III, V, I, VI, IV, II   B. V, I, IV, VI, II, III   C. III, IV, I, V, II, VI
   D. V, I, IV, VI, III, II   E. V, III, I, VI, IV, II

8. I. If, however, the rebuttal evidence presents an issue of credibility, it is for the jury to determine whether the presumption has, in fact, been destroyed.
    II. Once sufficient evidence to the contrary is introduced, the presumption disappears from the trial.
    III. The effect of a presumption is to place the burden upon the adversary to come forward with evidence to rebut the presumption.
    IV. When a presumption is overcome and ceases to exist in the case, the fact or facts which gave rise to the presumption still remain.
    V. Whether a presumption has been overcome is ordinarily a question for the court.
    VI. Such information may furnish a basis for a logical inference.
    The CORRECT answer is:
    A. IV, VI, II, V, I, III   B. III, II, V, I, IV, VI   C. V, III, VI, IV, II, I
    D. V, IV, I, II, VI, III   E. II, III, V, I, IV, VI

    8.____

9. I. An executive may answer a letter by writing his reply on the face of the letter itself instead of having a return letter typed.
    II. This procedure is efficient because it saves the executive's time, the typist's time, and saves office file space.
    III. Copying machines are used in small offices as well as large offices to save time and money in making brief replies to business letters.
    IV. A copy is made on a copying machine to go into the company files, while the original is mailed back to the sender.
    The CORRECT answer is:
    A. I, II, IV, III   B. I, IV, II, III   C. III, I, IV, II   D. III, IV, II, I

    9.____

10. I. Most organizations favor one of the types but always include the others to a lesser degree.
    II. However, we can detect a definite trend toward greater use of symbolic control.
    III. We suggest that our local police agencies are today primarily utilizing material control.
    IV. Control can be classified into three types: physical, material, and symbolic.
    The CORRECT answer is:
    A. IV, II, III, I   B. II, I, IV, III   C. III, IV, II, I   D. IV, I, III, II

    10.____

11. I. Project residents had first claim to this use, followed by surrounding neighborhood children.
    II. By contrast, recreation space within the project's interior was found to be used more often by both groups.
    III. Studies of the use of project grounds in many cities showed grounds left open for public use were neglected and unused, both by residents and by members of the surrounding community.
    IV. Project residents had clearly laid claim to the play spaces, setting up and enforcing unwritten rules for use.
    V. Each group, by experience, found their activities easily disrupted by other groups, and their claim to the use of space for recreation difficult to enforce.

    11.____

The CORRECT answer is:
A. IV, V, I, II, III
B. V, II, IV, III, I
C. I, IV, III, II, V
D. III, V, II, IV, I

12. I. They do not consider the problems correctable within the existing subsidy formula and social policy of accepting all eligible applicants regardless of social behavior.
    II. A recent survey, however, indicated that tenants believe these problems correctable by local housing authorities and management within the existing financial formula.
    III. Many of the problems and complaints concerning public housing management and design have created resentment between the tenant and the landlord.
    IV. This same survey indicated that administrators and managers do not agree with the tenants.
    The CORRECT answer is:
    A. II, I, III, IV   B. I, III, IV, II   C. III, II, IV, I   D. IV, II, I, III

13. I. In single-family residences, there is usually enough distance between tenants to prevent occupants from annoying one another.
    II. For example, a certain small percentage of tenant families has one or more members addicted to alcohol.
    III. While managers believe in the right of individuals to live as they choose, the manager becomes concerned when the pattern of living jeopardizes others' rights.
    IV. Still others turn night into day, staging lusty entertainments which carry on into the hours when most tenants are trying to sleep.
    V. In apartment buildings, however, tenants live so closely together that any misbehavior can result in unpleasant living conditions.
    VI. Other families engage in violent argument.
    The CORRECT answer is:
    A. III, II, V, IV, VI, I
    B. I, V, II, VI, IV, III
    C. II, V, IV, I, III, VI
    D. IV, II, V, VI, III, I

14. I. Congress made the commitment explicit in the Housing Act of 194, establishing as a national goal the realization of a *decent home and suitable environment for every American family*.
    II. The result has been that the goal of decent home and suitable environment is still as far distant as ever for the disadvantaged urban family.
    III. In spite of this action by Congress, federal housing programs have continued to be fragmented and grossly underfunded.
    IV. The passage of the National Housing Act signaled a few federal commitment to provide housing for the nation's citizens.
    The CORRECT answer is:
    A. I, IV, III, II   B. IV, I, III, II   C. IV, I, II, III   D. II, IV, I, III

15.
I. The greater expense does not necessarily involve *exploitation*, but it is often perceived as exploitative and unfair by those who are aware of the price differences involved, but unaware of operating costs.
II. Ghetto residents believe they are *exploited* by local merchants, and evidence substantiates some of these beliefs.
III. However, stores in low-income areas were more likely to be small independents, which could not achieve the economies available to supermarket chains and were, therefore, more likely to charge higher prices, and the customers were more likely to buy smaller-sized packages which are more expensive per unit of measure.
IV. A study conducted in one city showed that distinctly higher prices were charged for goods sold in ghetto stores in other areas.

The CORRECT answer is:
  A. IV, II, I, III   B. IV, I, III, II   C. II, IV, III, I   D. II, III, IV, I

15._____

KEY (CORRECT ANSWERS)

1.	C	6.	C	11.	D
2.	E	7.	A	12.	C
3.	B	8.	B	13.	B
4.	B	9.	C	14.	B
5.	D	10.	D	15.	C

PREPARING WRITTEN MATERIALS
EXAMINATION SECTION
TEST 1

DIRECTIONS: Each question or incomplete statement is followed by several suggested answers or completions. Select the one that BEST answers the question or completes the statement. *PRINT THE LETTER OF THE CORRECT ANSWER IN THE SPACE AT THE RIGHT.*

Questions 1-25.

DIRECTIONS: Questions 1 through 25 consist of sentences which may or may not be examples of good English usage. Consider grammar, punctuation, spelling, capitalization, awkwardness, etc. Examine each sentence and then choose the correct statement about it from the four choices below it. If the English usage in the sentence given is better than it would be with any of the changes suggested in options B, C, and D, choose option A. Do not choose an option that will change the meaning of the sentence.

1. According to Judge Frank, the grocer's sons found guilty of assault and sentenced last Thursday.
    A. This is an example of acceptable writing.
    B. A comma should be placed after the word *sentenced*.
    C. The word *were* should be placed after *sons*.
    D. The apostrophe in grocer's should be placed after the *s*.

1.____

2. The department heads assistant said that the stenographers should type duplicate copies of all contracts, leases, and bills.
    A. This is an example of acceptable writing,
    B. A comma should be placed before the word "*contracts*.
    C. An apostrophe should be placed before the *s* in *heads*.
    D. Quotation marks should be placed before the *stenographers* and after *bills*.

2.____

3. The lawyers questioned the men to determine who was the true property owner?
    A. This is an example of acceptable writing.
    B. The phrase *questioned the men* should be changed to *asked the men questions*.
    C. The word *was* should be changed to *were*.
    D. The question mark should be changed to a period.

3.____

119

4. The terms stated in the present contract are more specific than those stated in the previous contract.
   A. This is an example of acceptable writing,
   B. The word *are* should be changed to *is*.
   C. The word *than* should be changed to *then*.
   D. The word *specific* should be changed to *specified*.

   4.____

5. Of the few lawyers considered, the one who argued more skillful was chosen for the job.
   A. This is an example of acceptable writing.
   B. The word *more* should be replaced by the word *most*.
   C. The word *skillful* should be replaced by the word *skillfully*.
   D. The word *chosen* should be replaced by the word *selected*.

   5.____

6. Each of the states has a court of appeals; some states have circuit courts.
   A. This is an example of acceptable writing
   B. The semi-colon should be changed to a comma.
   C. The word *has* should be changed to *have*.
   D. The word *some* should be capitalized.

   6.____

7. The court trial has greatly effected the child's mental condition.
   A. This is an example of acceptable writing.
   B. The word *effected* should be changed to *affected*.
   C. The word *greatly* should be placed after *effected*.
   D. The apostrophe in *child's* should be placed after the *s*.

   7.____

8. Last week, the petition signed by all the officers was sent to the Better Business Bureau.
   A. This is an example of acceptable writing.
   B. The phrase *last week* should be placed after *officers*.
   C. A comma should be placed after *petition*.
   D. The word *was* should be changed to *were*.

   8.____

9. Mr. Farrell claims that he requested form A-12, and three booklets describing court procedures.
   A. This is an example of acceptable writing.
   B. The word *that* should be eliminated.
   C. A colon should be placed after *requested*.
   D. The comma after *A-12* should be eliminated.

   9.____

10. We attended a staff conference on Wednesday the new safety and fire rules were discussed.
    A. This is an example of acceptable writing.
    B. The words *safety, fire,* and *rules* should begin with capital letters.
    C. There should be a comma after the word *Wednesday*.
    D. There should be a period after the word *Wednesday*, and the word *the* should begin with a capital letter.

    10.____

11. Neither the dictionary or the telephone directory could be found in the office library.
    A. This is an example of acceptable writing.
    B. The word *or* should be changed to *nor*.
    C. The word *library* should be spelled *libery*.
    D. The word *neither* should be changed to *either*.

11._____

12. The report would have been typed correctly if the typist could read the draft.
    A. This is an example of acceptable writing.
    B. The word *would* should be removed.
    C. The word *have* should be inserted after the word *could*.
    D. The word *correctly* should be changed to *correct*.

12._____

13. The supervisor brought the reports and forms to an employees desk.
    A. This is an example of acceptable writing.
    B. The word *brought* should be changed to *took*.
    C. There should be a comma after the word *reports* and a comma after the word *forms*.
    D. The word *employees* should be spelled *employee's*.

13._____

14. It's important for all the office personnel to submit their vacation schedules on time.
    A. This is an example of acceptable writing.
    B. The word *It's* should be spelled *Its*.
    C. The word *their* should be spelled *they're*.
    D. The word *personnel* should be spelled *personal*.

14._____

15. The supervisor wants that all staff members report to the office at 9:00 A.M.
    A. This is an example of acceptable writing.
    B. The word *that* should be removed and the word *to* should be inserted after the word *members*.
    C. There should be a comma after the word *wants* and a comma after the word *office*.
    D. The word *wants* should be changed to *want* and the word *shall* should be inserted after the word *members*.

15._____

16. Every morning the clerk opens the office mail and distributes it.
    A. This is an example of acceptable writing.
    B. The word *opens* should be changed to *letters*.
    C. The word *mail* should be changed to *letters*.
    D. The word *it* should be changed to *them*.

16._____

17. The secretary typed more fast on a desktop computer than on a tablet.
    A. This is an example of acceptable writing.
    B. The words *more fast* should be changed to *faster*.
    C. There should be a comma after the words *desktop computer*.
    D. The word *than* should be changed to *then*.

17._____

18. The typist used an extention cord in order to connect her typewriter to the outlet nearest to her desks.
    A. This is an example of acceptable writing.
    B. A period should be placed after the word *cord*, and the word *in* should have a capital *I*.
    C. A comma should be placed after the word *typewriter*.
    D. The word *extention* should be spelled *extension*.

19. He would have went to the conference if he had received an invitation.
    A. This is an example of acceptable writing.
    B. The word *went* should be replaced by the word *gone*.
    C. The word *had* should be replaced by *would have*.
    D. The word *conference* should be spelled *conferance*.

20. In order to make the report neater, he spent many hours rewriting it.
    A. This is an example of acceptable writing.
    B. The word *more* should be inserted before the word *neater*.
    C. There should be a colon after the word *neater*.
    D. The word *spent* should be changed to *have spent*.

21. His supervisor told him that he should of read the memorandum more carefully.
    A. This is an example of acceptable writing.
    B. The word *memorandum* should be spelled *memorandom*.
    C. The word *of* should be replaced by the word *have*.
    D. The word *carefully* should be replaced by the word *careful*.

22. It was decided that two separate reports should be written.
    A. This is an example of acceptable writing.
    B. A comma should be inserted after the word *decided*.
    C. The word *be* should be replaced by the word *been*.
    D. A colon should be inserted after the word *that*.

23. She don't seem to understand that the work must be done as soon as possible.
    A. This is an example of acceptable writing.
    B. The word *doesn't* should replace the word *don't*.
    C. The word *why* should replace the word *that*.
    D. The word *as* before the word *soon* should be eliminated.

24. He excepted praise from his supervisor for a job well done.
    A. This is an example of acceptable writing.
    B. The word *excepted* should be spelled *accepted*.
    C. The order of the words *well done* should be changed to *done well*.
    D. There should be a comma after the word *supervisor*.

25. What appears to be intentional errors in grammar occur several times in the passage.   25._____
    A. This is an example of acceptable writing.
    B. The word *occur* should be spelled *occur*.
    C. The word *appears* should be changed to *appear*.
    D. The phrase *several times* should be changed to *from time to time*.

KEY (CORRECT ANSWERS)

1.	C	11.	B
2.	C	12.	C
3.	D	13.	D
4.	A	14.	A
5.	C	15.	B
6.	A	16.	A
7.	B	17.	B
8.	A	18.	D
9.	D	19.	B
10.	D	20.	A

21. C
22. A
23. B
24. B
25. C

TEST 2

DIRECTIONS: Each question consists of a sentence which may or may not be an example of good formal English usage. Examine each sentence, considering grammar, punctuation, spelling, capitalization, and awkwardness. Then choose the CORRECT statement about it from the four options below it. If the English usage in the sentence given is better than any of the changes suggested in options B, C, or D, pick option A. Do not pick an option that will change the meaning of the sentence. *PRINT THE LETTER OF THE CORRECT ANSWER IN THE SPACE AT THE RIGHT.*

1. I don't know who could possibly of broken it.
    A. This is an example of acceptable writing.
    B. The word *who* should be replaced by the word *whom*.
    C. The word *of* should be replaced by the word *have*.
    D. The word *broken* should be replaced by the word *broke*.

2. Telephoning is easier than to write.
    A. This is an example of acceptable writing.
    B. The word *telephoning* should be spelled *telephoneing*.
    C. The word *than* should be replaced by the word *then*.
    D. The words *to write* should be replaced by the word *writing*.

3. The two operators who have been assigned to these consoles are on vacation.
    A. This is an example of acceptable writing.
    B. A comma should be placed after the word *operators*.
    C. The word *who* should be replaced by the word *whom*.
    D. The word *are* should be replaced by the word *is*.

4. You were suppose to teach me how to operate a plugboard.
    A. This is an example of acceptable writing,
    B. The word *were* should be replaced by the word *was*.
    C. The word *suppose* should be replaced by the word *supposed*.
    D. The word *teach* should be replaced by the word *team*.

5. If you had taken my advice; you would have spoken with him.
    A. This is an example of acceptable writing.
    B. The word *advice* should be spelled *advise*.
    C. The words *had taken* should be replaced by the word *take*.
    D. The semicolon should be changed to a comma.

6. The clerk could have completed the assignment on time if he knows where these materials were located.
    A. This is an example of acceptable writing.
    B. The word *knows* should be replaced by *had known*.
    C. The word "were" should be replaced by *had been*.
    D. The words *where these materials were located* should be replaced by *the location of these materials*.

7. All employees should be given safety training. Not just those who have accidents.
    A. This is an example of acceptable writing,
    B. The period after the word *training* should be changed to a colon.
    C. The period after the word *training* should be changed to a semicolon, and the first letter of the word *Not* should be changed to a small *n*.
    D. The period after the word *training* should be changed to a comma, and the first letter of the word *Not* should be changed to a small *n*,

7._____

8. This proposal is designed to promote employee awareness of the suggestion program, to encourage employee participation in the program, and to increase the number of suggestions submitted.
    A. This is an example of acceptable writing.
    B. The word *proposal* should be spelled *proposal*.
    C. The words *to increase the number of suggestions submitted* should be changed to *an increase in the number of suggestions is expected*.
    D. The word *promote* should be changed to *enhance*, and the word *increase* should be changed to *add to*.

8._____

9. The introduction of inovative managerial techniques should be preceded by careful analysis of the specific circumstances and conditions in each department.
    A. This is an example of acceptable writing.
    B. The word *techniques* should be spelled *techneques*.
    C. The word *inovative* should be spelled *innovative*.
    D. A comma should be placed after the word *circumstances* and after the word *conditions*.

9._____

10. This occurrence indicates that such criticism embarrasses him.
    A. This is an example of acceptable writing.
    B. The word *occurrence* should be spelled *occurrence*.
    C. The word *criticism* should be spelled *creticism*.
    D. The word *embarrasses* should be spelled *embarasses*.

10._____

11. He can recommend a mechanic whose work is reliable.
    A. This is an example of acceptable writing.
    B. the word *reliable* should be spelled *relyable*.
    C. The word *whose* should be spelled *who's*.
    D. The word *mechanic* should be spelled *mecanic*.

11._____

12. She typed quickly; like someone who had not a moment to lose.
    A. This is an example of acceptable writing.
    B. The word *not* should be removed.
    C. The semicolon should be changed to a comma.
    D. The word *quickly* should be placed before instead of after the word *typed*.

12._____

13. She insisted that she had to much work to do. 13.____
    A. This is an example of acceptable writing.
    B. The word *insisted* should be spelled *insisted.*
    C. The word *to* used in front of *much* should be spelled *too.*
    D. The word *do* should be changed to *be done.*

14. The report, along with the accompanying documents, were submitted for 14.____
    review.
    A. This is an example of acceptable writing.
    B. The words *were submitted* should be changed to *was submitted.*
    C. The word *accompanying* should be spelled *accompaning.*
    D. The comma after the word *report* should be taken out.

15. If others must use your files, be certain that they understand how the system 15.____
    works, but insist that you do all the filing and refiling.
    A. This is an example of acceptable writing.
    B. There should be a period after the word *works*, and the word *but* should
       start a new sentence.
    C. The words *filing* and *refiling* should be spelled *fileing* and *refileing.*
    D. There should be a comma after the word *but.*

16. The appeal was not considered because of its late arrival. 16.____
    A. This is an example of acceptable writing.
    B. The word *its* should be changed to *it's.*
    C. The word *its* should be changed to *the.*
    D. The words *late arrival* should be changed to *arrival late.*

17. The letter must be read carefully to determine under which subject it should 17.____
    be filed.
    A. This is an example of acceptable writing.
    B. The word *under* should be changed to *at.*
    C. The word *determine* should be spelled *determin.*
    D. The word *carefully* should be spelled *carefuly.*

18. He showed potential as an office manager, but he lacked skill in delegating 18.____
    work.
    A. This is an example of acceptable writing.
    B. The word *delegating* should be spelled *delagating.*
    C. The word *potential* should be spelled *potencial.*
    D. The words *he lacked* should be changed to *was lacking.*

19. His supervisor told him that it would be all right to receive personal mail at 19.____
    the office.
    A. This is an example of acceptable writing.
    B. The words *all right* should be changed to *alright.*
    C. The word *personal* should be spelled *personel.*
    D. The word *mail* should be changed to *letters.*

20. The report, along with the accompanying documents, were submitted for review.   20._____
    A. This is an example of acceptable writing.
    B. The words *were submitted* should be changed to *was submitted*.
    C. The word *accompanying* should be spelled *accompaning*.
    D. The comma after the word *report* should be taken out.

KEY (CORRECT ANSWERS)

1.	C	11.	A
2.	D	12.	C
3.	A	13.	C
4.	C	14.	B
5.	D	15.	A
6.	B	16.	A
7.	D	17.	D
8.	A	18.	A
9.	C	19.	A
10.	A	20.	B

www.ingramcontent.com/pod-product-compliance
Lightning Source LLC
Chambersburg PA
CBHW081826300426
44116CB00014B/2501